SEVEN STEP
FENG
SHUI

LINA VISCONTI

SEVEN STEP FENG SHUI
by Lina Visconti

Copyright © 2000 by Lina Visconti

published by

TM Publications Worldwide
9251 Yonge Street, Unit 121
Richmond Hill, Ontario L4C 9T3

Library of Congress
Cataloging-in-Publication Data
Visconti, Lina
Seven Step Feng Shui, 2nd edition
Includes bibliographical references
ISBN 0-9684391-3-6 (pbk)
Desktop Publishing - Computer Publishing

© Cover design by Tom Mallioras
© Illustrations by Stephanie Rentel
© Photographs by Tom Mallioras, John Visconti and
Lina Visconti

Copyright 1998, 2000
First printing 1998
Second printing 2000, revised

Printed in Canada

For
Rick
John Mark
and Maryanne

ACKNOWLEDGMENTS

I would like to thank my parents, Fiorina and Mario Turco and my brothers and sisters Rose, John, Tony, Lorenzo, Ugo and Lidia for the colour in my life. I would also like to Rick, John Mark and Maryanne Visconti for their patience and support. Thank you to Stephanie Rentel for her brilliant artwork. Many thanks to Jennifer Volpe and Sheelagh Rutherford for their assistance in editing. A special thanks to Tom Mallioras for his dedication and patience in helping produce the new, bigger, better and improved edition of Seven Step Feng Shui.

INTRODUCTION

Feng Shui
An Ancient Guide To Successful Living

Feng Shui is an ancient Chinese system of creating balance in your environment. More than 5,000 years old it has now come of age. Introduced to the West about 100 years ago the basic principles of feng shui are as relevant today as they were then. Based on the five elements, the cycles of nature and the flow of energy feng shui can be seen as an all-embracing view of the universe connecting heaven, earth, and man. The scientific world acknowledges that our physical universe is not composed of matter but that its basic component is a kind of force or essence that we call energy. Although things may appear to be solid and separate from each other, on atomic and subatomic levels seemingly solid matter is seen as smaller and smaller particles. These fundamental particles are eventually reduced to just pure energy.

Physically we are all energy and everything around us is made up of energy. We are all part of one great energy field. Every molecule and atom, around and within us, vibrates at different rates of speed and has its own frequency and wavelength. We also know that energy is magnetic. Energy of a certain quality or vibration lends to attract onorgy of a similar quality and vibration. All forms of energy are interrelated and can affect one another.Energy has many different qualities from finer to denser. Thought, for example, is a fine, light form of energy and therefore easy to change. Matter, on the other hand, is dense compact energy and changes more slowly. All energy has both a positive and negative aspect. In feng shui this is seen as the polarities of yin and yang.It is the interaction between moving electrical charges and magnetic fields that is the underlying concept of feng shui. It shows us how to "tune in" to the energies around us so that we can live in harmony with our surroundings. Feng shui can influence and help change life situations such as your career, health, wealth, relationships and family life. It allows you to activate the powerful energies of the natural environment to work in your favour and guide you to successful living.

TABLE OF CONTENTS

CHAPTER ONE

WHAT IS FENG SHUI?

The name Feng Shui (pronounced Fung Shway) is based on two characters, Wind and Water. Often referred to as Chinese Geomancy, this ancient art of placement was used to locate the most harmonious surroundings to bury the dead and house the living. Proper site selection would bring luck to the descendants of the buried and would create harmonious living conditions for a home. In traditional Feng Shui the ideal location was chosen based on the observation of land formations, various earth energies, compass directions and ancient astrological charts. Perfect Feng Shui occurred when a location had lush vegetation, fertile soil, healthy wildlife, and protection from harsh winds and an adequate supply of fresh water - hence Feng Shui (Wind Water).

Feng Shui can be traced back to China as early as 618 AD. Core beliefs in Feng Shui were taken from ancient texts that dated as far back as the 4th Century. One such text was called the I Ching. This text was filled with predictions, complex language and symbolism, which was difficult to interpret. Feng Shui became a fine art that was limited to the

Emperor, his ministers and those who could read. After world War II, China was split in half by communism and Feng Shui was banished along with other feudal practices. Ancient texts were lost, stolen or destroyed and Feng Shui was only practiced in secret. Some of the ancient texts found their way across the water to Taiwan where Feng Shui practices were embraced and utilized both in residential and business spaces. It is no surprise that Taiwan is very rich in industry and trade.

Harnessing the earth's natural energies to create harmonious living conditions was not limited to China and Taiwan. Similar practices were soon discovered in many other parts of the world including India, South America and the Pacific Islands.

TAO

Feng Shui is based on philosophical principles of Taoism (pronounces DOWism) and referred to as Tao, "The Way". Chinese Taoism can be dated as far back as the 6th Century BC. Taoists see the cycles of nature and the constant change in the natural world as guides and the source of all things in the cosmos. They believe Heaven, earth and every living creature are connected to the whole in an interplay of action and reaction. Tao is to conduct one's life in harmony

Heaven, earth and every living creature are all connected to the whole in an interplay of action and reaction (Northern British Columbia)

without disrupting the natural scheme of things. To be in the Tao is to be connected and part of the whole.

YIN AND YANG

In Feng Shui the concept of yin and yang are terms to describe the flow of chi in the universe. Taoist tradition teaches that all things in the cosmos are based on two opposing yet complimentary principles called yin and yang. These forces contain a little of each in the other and are intertwined in a constant cyclic dance creating harmony and balance in all things. Yin is dark and still and while yang is light and in motion. The movement of planetary systems and the brightness of stars and suns balance the darkness of the universe. On earth daylight is yang while nighttime is yin. This system of opposites in harmony is used to evaluate the flow of energy in an environment. Traditional Feng Shui based land formations on the yin and yang systems. A tall mountain was yang while a deep valley was yin.

A place is balanced and has good Feng Shui when it is neither boring nor agitating but promotes the right level of arousal for the business at hand. Neither yin nor yang is ever 100% pure - one always contains a little of the other. All things contain varying degrees of yin and yang but a balance is most beneficial.

The principle of yin and yang can be utilized best by first determining what the purpose of the space is then decide whether to add or take away one or the other. As an example, if a bedroom's purpose is for sleeping only, then perhaps you may want to create more of a yin space. But then if a living room 's purpose is for socializing then adding more yang would add more energy. Some characteristics of yin and yang are listed below.

YIN	YANG
Dark	Light
Inward	Outward
Curved	Straight
Moon	Sun
Night	Day
Female	Male
Passive	Active
Cold	Hot
Death	Life
Low	High
Black	White
Receptive	Projective
Broken line	Solid line

FENG SHUI APPROACHES

It is said that there are many approaches to Feng Shui but in fact there are only two, the Form School and the Compass School. Practitioners combine one or both of these approaches with other practices such as energy reading, astrology, psychology, mythology and spiritualism, depending on the business at hand. There is no right or wrong approach to Feng Shui. Practitioners should consider geographical positioning in terms of land formation, spiritual and cultural beliefs as well as design limitations when applying their chosen approach.

YIN/YANG SYMBOL

The black portion of the symbol is yin or passive energy and the white represents yang or aggresive energy. The two are always in a constant state of flux and when in balance they are in harmony or tai chi. There is always a little yin inside the yang and a little yang inside the yin. Nothing is ever all yin or all yang.

FORM SCHOOL
*The Four Celestial Animals in an ideal setting
Tortoise in the north, Phoenix to the south,
Dragon in the east and Tiger in the west*

Form School

The form school of thought is based on land formations. Animals were used as a symbolic way of describing features in a landscape. A perfect location for a living environment would consist of four celestial animals positioned in what was often referred to as a classic armchair position.

The tortoise was a rounded hill that would be ideally protected a potential site from the winds of the north. On the west side of the site it was necessary to have the tiger in a yin or submissive position and to the east a large dragon in a yang or dominant position. The tiger and the dragon are representative of yin and yang creating perfect balance on either side of the site. Directly in front of the site the presence of an outstretched phoenix completed the land formations required for a well-balanced and harmonious living position.

Suitable abodes in auspicious locations would attract many settlers and develop into towns and cities. Soon, buildings and man made structures represented the symbolic dragon, tortoise, tiger and phoenix. As small towns and villages grew in population, the natural landscape was forever changed. To keep up with change other bodies of information were added. Astrology, geomancy, and mysticism

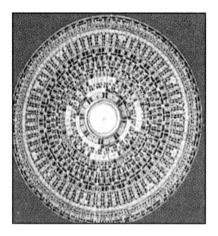

THE LOUPAN

The Loupan is a complex compass used by the Feng Shui Master. Originally the Lou Pan was hand made by the Feng Shui Master and contained their own formulas and secrets

were just a few influences that conttributed to the development of Feng Shui.

Compass School

The compass school of thought based its theories primarily on how a home was situated in relation to the stars in the solar system. A complex compass called a Loupan was developed to help the geomancer calculate data that would help discern appropriate directions to face a home or furniture and would also serve as an information system to calculate appropriate times to move, get married or have a child. In its entirety the system is extremely complex and it is an ancient technique, practiced by masters who have studied for dozens of years.

Modern Feng Shui

Today's Feng Shui experts base their practice on the underpinnings of Traditional Compass and Form School. A combination of other factors such as: cultural differences, spiritual beliefs, environmental changes, weather patterns and interior design are also taken into consideration.

CHI

Chi is the essence that is present in every element of the cosmos. It is the life force energy that propels everything into motion. Chi manifests itself in the atmosphere through gentle breezes or powerful winds, and on the earth through land formations such as mountains, hills and valleys. This vital power is inhaled and exhaled, it expands and condenses, it is mass or it can be vapor. When chi enters the depths of the earth and expands, it can erupt as in an active volcano, which is similar to a person consuming contaminated food and vomiting. In order for people to be healthy and prosperous the chi must be balanced and flow freely.

The Chinese have utilized the principles of chi for thousands of years. Martial artists demonstrate the power of chi via the powerful strike of a single hand movement. Acupuncturists use needles to tap into the body's meridians to unblock and balance chi.

If chi could be observed by the naked eye it would look like water moving in a stream or river. The ideal condition would be for the water to be gently meandering. Large rocks and excess debris in the water interrupt the flow and force erratic conditions. A straight path would cause the water to move quickly and rapidly to its destination. Water that is stuck in one spot with nowhere to go would eventually become stale and stagnate, creating a lifeless and noxious condition known as Sha Chi.

Recognizing and utilizing the positive flow of chi in an environment is a vital component of Feng Shui. A trained eye can tune in to and harness the natural pulses of the earth and stay clear of the negative energies that can cause ill effects.

Some of the factors that affect the flow of chi of an environment are as follows:

Vegetation

Healthy vegetation is the first and most important indicator of a location with good Feng Shui. Natural vegetation must be observed when considering a site on which to build. Dead or decayed branches on a tree can be a sign that the tree is diseased or has been affected by either wildlife or the weather. Stagnant water in the area contains harmful chemicals that destroy vegetation. Certain trees attract butterflies while others attract annoying insects such as mosquitoes. An awareness of the condition and type of vegetation may help select a sight that will bring positive chi into and around your home.

Pathways

A pathway can be defined as that which gets you from one point to another. The road that takes you to your destination will set feelings and attitudes into motion long before you arrive. Sidewalks, roads, driveways, footpaths, entranceways and hallways are all passages that lead you from one experience to another. The energy you feel during the journey will depend on whether the pathway is long and narrow, bright and cheerful or bumpy and crowded. Consider the most relaxing path you ever walked upon and the most nerve-racking plane ride you have taken.

Placement of Furniture and Objects

How and where objects are placed in a space can have a profound effect on the inhabitants of the space. Furniture placed too closely together creates the same feeling as a crowded elevator - stuffy with no air to breathe. Furniture should always be placed in such a way that it is easy to navigate. As a rule sofas, chairs and beds should always have an unimpaired view of the doorway. Paintings and other objects should be carefully analyzed as to their meaning before being displayed in key locations. A painting of a violent storm with waves crashing against the rocks may cause restless sleep, if located on a bedroom wall.

Maintenance

Keeping a home and its contents in good repair and in working order is a reflection of how you feel about yourself. Uncut grass, overgrown weeds and dead plants around your home give the impression of abandonment and neglect. Cracked driveways, walkways and windows catch Sha chi between the cracks creating a sense of old age and staleness. A leaky faucet could mean your wealth is going down the drain. Broken appliances, objects and furniture attract negative energy and should either be fixed or thrown out.

Clutter

Everything is attached to you with a constantly tugging string. Clutter is one of the main causes of stale energy in and around a home. When chi enters your home it can get stuck in crowded corners, over-stuffed closets, over-filled drawers or on messy counter tops. A good rule to follow is if you don't like it, don't need it or haven't used it in two years, get rid of it. Clearing clutter is one of the first and most important steps in practicing successful Feng Shui.

Poison Arrows

A poison arrow is like the cutting edge of a blade - pointed in your direction. A poison arrow can be a tall hydro pole located directly in front of your doorway, greeting you each day as you step outside, or a tall building looming over your home. Beams across a ceiling that create a heavy oppressed feeling can also be considered poison arrows. When two sharp edges meet they cause negative energy and are also considered poison arrows.

Blocks

In Feng Shui a block is that which stops or inter-rupts the flow of chi. If a tree or branch fell across your driveway then its removal would be necessary. Overgrown trees blocking the view from a window or masking the entrance to your home are examples of blocks. Inside your home, excessive or oversized furniture in a small room can impede or smother the flow of chi.

Electromagnetic Fields

The subtle energy given off by overhead power lines, transformer boxes, electric blankets, small appliances, televisions and computers is a proven health risk with long periods of exposure. Although it is difficult to avoid using modern appliances such as blow dryers or computers it is important to realize that all of these create magnetic fields that can affect your well being. Electromagnetic fields cannot be seen by the naked eye, however, as indicated by car radio static and interference, they are always surrounding us.

CHAPTER TWO

I CHING
THE BOOK OF CHANGES

THE I CHING

The I Ching is an ancient Chinese book of divination and wisdom that gives you amazingly accu-
rate insights into life. Possibly the oldest book in the
world it is believed to have been written over 6000
years ago. Miraculously it escaped the burning of
books under the tyrant Emperor Chin Shih Huang Ti to
become the center core of Chinese philosophy.
Many great sages including Confucius have used the
I Ching as the basis for their teachings and educa-
tion.

The actual origins of the I Ching have been lost
in the mists of time. It is thought by some to have
been written by a combination of people over a period of many years. Others believe it was left by an
alien civilization. Whatever its beginnings it has been
used through the ages as a tool to help us understand what the universe is saying to us.

The universe is made up of two primal forces of
passive and active energy or chi. These two yin and
yang forces are constantly in a dynamic play of

action and reaction. The symbol that illustrates these forces is known as tai chi. Yin and yang forces are divided into the eight trigrams known as the Pa Kua grid. Pa means eight and Kua means trigram. Each trigram represents a force of nature in its passive yin or active yang stage and illustrates how everything in our universe is interconnected. These trigrams are made up of three lines that are either solid (yang) or broken (yin). Each trigram is associated with a compass direction, colour, sound, number, family member and element.

The eight trigrams are then multiplied by themselves to form 64 hexigrams or life changes. These 64 hexigrams can help us deal with changes in our lives by providing advice which offers insight into any situation. It is interesting to note that the 64 hexigrams of the I Ching are the same as those of the genetic code which consists of 64 triplets of nucleotides called codons. Another fascinating connection is that the patterns found in the I Ching mirror the mathematical patterns found in the binary system. The binary code is a two number base system which is used in every computer calculation performed today. Yin and yang symbols are simply another way of counting in two's.

The more you know about the I Ching the more

you will come to appreciate the wisdom of it's teachings. For centuries the I Ching oracle has been used to communicate with the spiritual forces of the universe. Consulting the I Ching helps develop and trust your own intuitive insights. Often it confirms what you may already be thinking and other times it gives new information. There are times when the insight your receive is not pleasing, however, let the information be absorbed in your mind and you may quickly discover it's hidden value.

There are various means of consulting with the I Ching ranging from drawing straws to tossing coins. In this book we will demonstrate the coin tossing method so that you too can gain insight into this valuable method of divination. This section provides a mini version of the I Ching hexigrams and based on the author's interpretation. It is strongly recommended that you pick up your a copy of the I Ching. Brian Browne Walker's publication of the I Ching is by far one of the best interpretations available today (ISBN 0312-09828-06)

THE EIGHT TRIGRAMS

NAME	SYMBOL	FAMILY MEMBER	DIRECTION	ELEMENT	NUMBER	CHARACTERISTIC
CH'IEN	HEAVEN	FATHER	NORTHWEST	METAL	6	CREATIVE, VITALITY
CHEN	THUNDER	OLDEST SON	EAST	WOOD	3	AROUSAL, MOVEMENT
K'AN	WATER	MIDDLE SON	NORTH	WATER	1	FLOWING, DANGER
KEN	MOUNTAIN	YOUNGEST SON	NORTHEAST	EARTH	8	STILLNESS, STEADINESS
K'UN	EARTH	MOTHER	SOUTHWEST	EARTH	2	RECEPTIVE, YIELDING
SUN	WIND	OLDEST DAUGHTER	SOUTHEAST	WOOD	4	GENTLENESS, PENETRATION
LI	FIRE	MIDDLE DAUGHTER	SOUTH	FIRE	9	DEPENDENCE,
TUI	LAKE	YOUNGEST DAUGHTER	WEST	METAL	7	JOY, SERENITY

I CHING DIVINATION

Before you begin take a few minutes to ponder on a question that you would like insight into (it cannot be a simple yes/no question). You will need a simple coin and a pen and paper. The coin is tossed a total of six times, each throw representing either yang (solid line) or yin (broken line). Heads is equal to a YANG line where tails will be a YIN line. Record your throws by drawing either a yin or yang line for each throw. Begin drawing your lines from the bottom and work your way up to the top. You will end up with a series of six lines that are a combo of yin or yang. The bottom three lines are the bottom trigram where the top three lines are the top trigram. Each trigram represents an element from nature such as water, fire, earth, mountain, wind, lake, thunder. Refer to the chart below. Locate the top trigram and the bottom trigram. The place on the chart that they meet refers to a hexagram number. Look up the number and refer to your insight. If the insight does not make sense, just refer back to it later in the day. The I Ching can be consulted on a daily basis or as needed.

HOW TO THROW COINS

List the numbers one to six starting at the bottom. Throw the first coin, if it is heads draw a solid (yang) line and if it is tails draw a broken (yin) line. Do this six times each time drawing a solid or broken line. Your throw should look similar to the sample shown on the right. The top three lines are the fire trigram and the bottom is known as water. Refer to the hexagram chart and identify top triagram and bottom tri-grams. You will find a number on the point where they meet and find your number. In the sample below the number is #64.

```
6  ──────    Top set
5  ──  ──    Fire
4  ──────
```

```
3  ──  ──    Bottom set
2  ──────    Water
1  ──  ──
```

HEXAGRAM SELECTION CHART
match upper trigram with lower trigram

UPPER ➤ / LOWER ▼	Heaven ☰	Thunder ☳	Water ☵	Mountain ☶	Earth ☷	Wind ☴	Fire ☲	Lake ☱
Heaven ☰	1	34	5	26	11	9	14	43
Thunder ☳	25	51	3	27	24	42	21	17
Water ☵	6	40	29	4	7	59	64	47
Mountain ☶	33	62	39	52	15	53	56	31
Earth ☷	12	16	8	23	2	20	35	45
Wind ☴	44	32	48	18	46	57	50	28
Fire ☲	13	55	63	22	36	37	30	49
Lake ☱	10	54	60	41	19	61	38	58

1. CHIEN

HEAVEN *above*

HEAVEN *below*

Creative power is available to you. An abundant source of power from the universe is now available to you, all you need to do is tap into it. Be receptive and but make no hasty decisions. Meditate and let a higher power be your guide.

2. KUN

EARTH *above*

EARTH *below*

This is a time to follow rather than lead. Be receptive and let nourishment flow your way. Assist rather than initiate. Listen to others and hear what they are saying. Time for you to be silent and let others do the talking. Step back, take a deep breath be open, fair and unbiased.

3. CHUN

WATER *above*

THUNDER *below*

Like the blade of grass trying to make it's way through a crack in the cement so must you persevere and be tough. Don't give up because out of the dark you will see the sun shine and the beginning of new things to come. A chick needs to break through it's own shell if it is to survive and be strong. See and respect the council of others that are pure of heart.

4. MING

MOUNTAIN *above*

WATER *below*

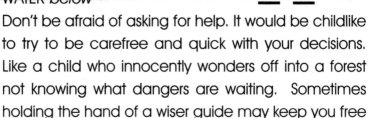

Don't be afraid of asking for help. It would be childlike to try to be carefree and quick with your decisions. Like a child who innocently wonders off into a forest not knowing what dangers are waiting. Sometimes holding the hand of a wiser guide may keep you free from harm and teach you the wisdom you need to survive.

5. HSU

WATER *above*

HEAVEN *below*

Do not force things to happen. Waiting is the key to success. Keep a stiff upper lip, be patient and keep a positive attitude. Be mindful of inner truths and keep you inner strengh. Do not doubt yourself and make a desperate decision. Wait for a higher power to help you do the right thing.

6. SUNG

HEAVEN *above*

WATER *below*

There is conflict in your life at this time. Whether it is internal or with others doesn't matter. The best thing for you to do is to try to remove yourself and your thoughts away from the situation. Find solitude and meditate until your thoughts become pure and clear. Sometimes the best thing to do is nothing.

7. SHIH
EARTH *above*
WATER *below*

Conduct yourself properly when faced with adversity. If your superior has achieved a position by force then he/she will not last long and he/she will quickly lose the support of everyone around them. If however your superior has achieved a position based on knowledge and fairness he/she will endure and you must give he/she your support.

8. PI
WATER *above*
EARTH *below*

It is a time for sticking together with those that are close to you. Like water and earth go together and create life you must complement and assist one another. Inner truth, balance and genuine concern will guide you to good fortune.

9. HSIAO CH'U
WIND *above*
HEAVEN below

This is a good time to hold back. No matter how valiant your efforts may be it will not be fruitful for you. It is not a good time to start a new business or new projects. Take a few steps back and look forward without taking action, then move forward by taking a few small steps at a time.

10. LU
HEAVEN *above*
LAKE *below*

Take cautious gentle steps in resolving conflict. Do not loose your temper. Remain calm and use integrity and courtesy especially in business practices. More will be gained by using dignity and respect. When negative energy comes your way try to stay quiet and gently walk the other way.

11. T'AI
EARTH *above*
HEAVEN *below*

See yourself as a young plant growing upwards towards the heavens. Be aware of the ground that nourishes you and feeds you and at the same time reach for the sky. Know that your basic needs will sustain you while at the same time focusing on moving and progressing upwards towards a higher self.

12. P'I
HEAVEN *above*
EARTH *below*

Inferior influences prevail while spiritual life begins to descend. You may feel like you are stagnating and those around you also seek to express these feeings. Turn inwards and be silent. Meditate and focus on your inner higher self and seek guidance so that balance may be restored.

13. T'UNG JEN

HEAVEN *above*

FIRE *below*

Cultivate relationships with others. Relationships must be conduced in the open. Practice fair, honest and sincere attitudes towards others and treat them like you would like to be treated. Your intentions should be clear and there should be no hidden agendas with your relationships at home, work or play.

14. TA YU

FIRE *above*

HEAVEN *below*

You are being influenced by a higher power. Creativity is surrounding you in all aspects of your life. Remain modest, clear and balanced and good things will come your way. You increase your personal power by purifying your thoughts actions and attitudes. Do not become over confident in the ability to control events or the tides may change.

15. CH'IEN

EARTH *above*

MOUNTAIN *below*

Remain modest and not boisterous, arrogant and egotistical. Retain modesty and become loved and respected by all. Hold on to your innocence, sincerity and openess in every situation. Empty your self and prepare to receive blessings from a higher power.

16. YU

THUNDER *above*

EARTH *below*

Enthusiasm can either lead to misfortune or success. If your enthusiasm comes from proper sources then you will surely recieve rewards. If the enthusiasm is ego based it can be fasle and misleading and may lead to misfortune. Proper enthusiasm is obtained from inner balance and inner truths.

17. SUI

LAKE *above*

THUNDER *below*

Devote yourself to inner truths and others will be loyal and follow you. Accept the way things are even though you may not agree with the circumstances. Stay away from courageous endevours, rather let others take the lead in this situtation.

18. KU

MOUNTAIN *above*

WIND *below*

There is a defect in your attitude or in society that needs to be addressed at this time. This problem may appear to be one that does not have resolve. Do not abandon it as a solution is close at hand. The defect will be elimated by using gentleness rather than harshness. Spend several days reflecting, solving and ensuring that the problem does not return.

19. LIN

EARTH *above*

LAKE *below*

Stay within the path of truth as there are powerful influences coming your way. These influences will bring you closer to success and abundance. New goals should be pursued right away. Accept what comes your way with modesty and humility and enjoy your prosperity.

20. KUAN

WIND *above*

EARTH *below*

Set an example for others through your actions. Study the I Ching and you tap into the underlying principles of the universe. Through the contemplation of principles such as modesty, acceptance and tolerance you will set an example for others to follow.

21. SHIH HO

FIRE *above*

THUNDER *below*

Trust has been broken by another. Aggressive action may result in misfortune. Withdraw and go into meditation and seek advise from higher powers. It is not for us to punish others for their wrongful doings. Remove yourself from the situation and things will works themselves out.

22. PI
MOUNAIN *above*
FIRE *below*

Do not use forceful ways to get what you want, especially from others. You may feel empowered for the moment but this is only temporary. Success only comes from the gentleness of internal forces. Draw on inner knowledge and truth instead of being forceful. Proper conduct brings great rewards.

23. PO
MOUNTAIN *above*
EARTH *below*

Your situation at this time is descending. Inferior influences are prevelent and nothing that you can do will stop this from happening. The sun always shines after the clouds are gone. When such times come we feel anxious and depressed. Do not doubt yourself or be fearfull and most of all don't lose your faith. Try to look for the good that will come from the situation.

24. FU
EARTH *above*
THUNDER *below*

The clouds have passed and you are beginning to see the light. Things will begin to change for you. Do not force things to go any faster. Things happen in their own time. Take a rest, replenish yourself and get ready for the good things coming your way.

25. WU WANG

HEAVEN *above*
THUNDER *below*

Do not let your ego stand in the way of pure guidance from the divine spirit within. When ego takes over we tend to get ahead of ourselves without listening to the truth within. Being ambitious and making quick descisions will lead you down the wrong path. Taking time to listen to our inner feelings (intuiton) will give you the proper insights.

26. TA CH'U

MOUNTAIN *above*
HEAVEN *below*

Great power has come your way. Cultivate this opportunity and use it to achieve a higher good. It is a time of challenge and possible pressure. Keep true to your principles and keep your integrity while others look for weaknesses in you. It is a good time to start on a new project.

27. I

MOUNTAIN *above*
THUNDER *below*

This is a good time to improve your eating habits. Time to provide better nourishment to both your body and spirit. What you put into your body affects your spirit. A healthy outward appearance creates positive energy which in turn leads you to better fortune.

28. TA KUO

LAKE *above*

WIND *below*

You are capable of achieving much success. An enormous amount of energy is waiting for you. Let it in a little at a time and direct it to where it will be most useful. You may want to spread it out into a few different projects rather than sending it all in one direction. Do not let it sit too long or like a damn that holds back the water - it may burst open and you will lose control.

29. K'AN

WATER *above*

WATER *below*

This is a time of possible danger. It may seem like you are falling and there is no way out. Be confident and keep your virtue. Don't try to fight, just go with the flow and things will work out.

30. LI

FIRE *above*

FIRE *below*

Your own efforts together with the help of others can help you achieve more success than you can imagine. Enlist the help of others rather than trying on your own. In times of good and bad challenges we need to be dependent on others especially friends and family. Do this and fortune will come your way.

31. HSIEN

LAKE *above*

MOUNTAIN *below*

There is an influence coming your way. It can be pleasing or it can be disruptive, depending on how you receive it. You will attract what you think about. If you have attracted a disruptive challenge then you should persevere and attempt to resolve it in a gentle and kind manner. Handling this influence properly may lead to a lasting relationship.

32. HENG

THUNDER *above*

WIND *below*

Move forward with what you are doing. Don't allow your ego to take over and boast on your successes. Don't expect too much too soon. Hold steady and move ahead holding true to your inner truth. If you are consistant with your actions you will succeed.

33. TUN

HEAVEN *above*

MOUNTAIN *below*

Responding properly to things that anger you will be the key to your success. Sometimes the best response is no response. Your silence is a response within itself. Withdraw into the safety of stillness while others are all running around and reacting emotionally. In the silence you will find the answer.

34. TA CHUANG

THUNDER *above*

HEAVEN *below*

Ego based power and greatness leads to false identiy. Influence is obtained by first purifying your thoughts and emotions. Do not judge or condemn, punish or manipulate others for the purpose of attaining your own greatness. Honesty and integrity are the keys to being a strong leader. You are as strong as those who follow you.

35. CHIN

FIRE *above*

EARTH *below*

You have come a long way. This is a time of easy progress providing you keep on consulting with your higher self. You are in a position to reap great benefits. Increase your social circle and align yourself with those who will support you. In turn you must respect them and give them credit where credit is due.

36. MING

EARTH *above*

FIRE *below*

This is a time for you to slow down and be silent. The present circumstances are now enveloped in the dark so look to the light within yourself. Do not avoid or force the light in. Do not allow yourself to become negative. Let the higher power lead to you.

37. CHIA JEN

WIND *above*

FIRE *below*

Concern yourself with the state of your family and home life. Priority lies within the family and in order for all things to be in harmony around you must first strengthen the family unit. Love, honour and dedication at home will lead to success outside the home.

38. K'UEI

FIRE *above*

LAKE *below*

There are many situations in life that lead us to think negative thoughts. Fear of failure or fear of success may lead you to doubt yourself. You may need to reflect on these things at this time and trust that it is for a reason even though it may not be clear. Lessons are needed before moving to the next stage.

39. CHIEN

WATER *above*

MOUNTAIN *below*

You are in the middle of a tough situation and possibly surrounded by obstacles. Desire, fear and anger are emotions that are tempting you but don't give in. Think about your challenge before making any type of emotional decision. Meditate and try to balance yourself by making the necesary corrections so that you can remove the blocks and feel clear.

40. HSIEH

THUNDER *above*

WATER *below*

A change of attitude is needed before you are deliv-
ered from tension and difficulty.   Difficulties and
obstacles are sometimes necessary to learn lessons
but once learned we can go on to resolve personal
and social conflicts.

41. SUN

MOUNTAIN *above*

LAKE *below*

Resources are limited at this time.   Do not become
angry or unhappy, rather look at it as a time to clear,
release and even cut back on unnecessary luxuries.
The lesson you will learn from this will help you to
become stronger, wiser and more creative in your
day to day activities.

42. I

WIND *above*

THUNDER *below*

More power is upon you and its a time where your life
will be invigorated.   Opportunity and advancement is
close at hand.   Act quickly and enlist the help of others so that you may achieve important goals.
Respect and honour those that help you so that they
too can become empowered at this time.

43. KUAI

LAKE *above*

HEAVEN *below*

A concern that has hovered over you for a long period of time is now about to dissolve. Change is close at hand. Do not sit back and get too relaxed as there is still much to be done. In order to remain free of difficulties in the future you must push forward by doing what is righteousness and good for all involved.

44. KOU

HEAVEN *above*

WIND *below*

You are in danger of letting your dark side seduce you and make false promises. You must resist the temptation or misfortune will come your way. Examine motives that are of a questionable nature. Be still and draw on your intuition to guide you in the right direction.

45. TS'UI

LAKE *above*

EARTH *below*

Before we can achieve harmony and balance on a large scale we must first look in our own backyards. Create harmony and balance with your own family, friends and community and by doing so the goodness of your actions spread far beyond your reaches.

46. SHENG

EARTH *above*
WIND *below*

Great progress can be made at this time if you are open to guidance from a teacher. Ask for help from those that are willing to give it to you. Cultivate inner strength and independence and at the same time trust in a wiser sage who can help you move upwards.

47. K'UN

LAKE *above*
WATER *below*

Exhaustion and oppression at one time or other is simply a way of life. Meeting these challenges with a positive spirit will help you meet with success at a later date. Say little, do little and be gentle towards others. Take this time to rest, meditate and balance yourself.

48. CHING

WATER *above*
WIND *below*

Communities cannot survive without a healthy source of water. No human can survive without a healthy spirit. Just as you seek pure, clean fresh water to quench your thirst so should you seek out guidance and insights through the I Ching to nourish your spirit.

49. KO

LAKE *above*

FIRE *below*

It is time to move away from a stagnant situation and make room for something new. Go inward for guidance and clarity. Do not be hastful and make rash descisions. Seek guidance from a higher power and enlist the help of others that you trust.

50. TING

FIRE *above*

WIND *below*

Taking charge and making aggressive demands may not be the best way to succeed. It would be far wiser to listen carefully to a wise sage. Go inward and allow the inner mind to guide you with clarity and truth.

51. CHEN

THUNDER *above*

THUNDER *below*

The universe must sometimes use shocking events to set us back on the right path. Sometimes a bolt of lightning will help us realize that we need to stop and analyse our ways and perhaps make some adjustments. It is also a time to acknowledge other powers that are much greater than us.

52. KEN

MOUNTAIN *above*

MOUNTAIN *below*

Take some time to clear your mind and be still. It is not a good time to make hasty decisions with regards to goals and especially relationships. Moving away from your emotions will help you to think more clearly. Meditate and excercise the law of non doing for the time being.

53. CHIEN

WIND *above*

MOUNTAIN *below*

Just like a tree needs to properly root itself before it grows upwards it is necessary to first ground yourself before reaching for the sky. A proper foundation takes time and patience. Moving too quickly will lead to instability and misfortune.

54. KUEI MEI

THUNDER *above*

LAKE *below*

Stay focussed on your long term plans. Although your ideas and actions may not be appreciated and may even be rejected do not force action or acceptance. Be passive and do not attract attention to yourself. The timing is not right at the moment.

55. FENG
THUNDER *above*
FIRE *below*

This is a time of abundance and power. It is short lived and can bring fortune your way. Seek the help of others and they too will benefit from the abundance. If you are not certain and cannot approach the moment with a clear mind and pure intention then let it go and wait for another time.

56. LU
FIRE *above*
MOUNTAIN *below*

This is a period of transition. Anything you attempt including relationships may be temporary. Go with the flow of things and keep moving knowing that this is only temporary. Learn from each encounter and move on to the next challenge.

57. SUN
WIND *above*
WIND *below*

Be clear of your goal and focus on going in one direction. If you aren't clear you may be going in too many directions and not getting anyware. Once the direction is clear you can put your full force into it and give it the power it needs. Be sincere and true to your ideals and you will be successful.

58. TUI

LAKE *above*

LAKE *below*

Learn the art of giving and receiving. Aggressive action and ego is not the way to achieve joy and success. What is won by the ego will not last. Friendliness and sincere effort and the ability to share with others will be your key to long lasting happiness and success.

59. HUAN

WIND *above*

WATER *below*

There are indications that harshness and rigidity is present within yourself or in others around you. Now is the time to work things out and resolve disputes. It is a time to forgive and lean towards a gentle and caring attitude.

60. CHIEH

WATER *above*

LAKE *below*

It is a time to practice being a little more practical both in a material and spiritual sense. It is a time to take a look at the whole picture and create balance and order by trimming away what is of no use. Set wise limits on your spending and it will pay off in the long run.

61. CHUNG FU

WIND *above*

LAKE *below*

Solving difficult situations can be done if you search for inner truth. Put aside strong emotional reaction and be silent within yourself. Allow your inner spirit to give you guidance so that you can find the best solutution.

62. HSIAO KUA

THUNDER *above*

MOUNTAIN *below*

You are in difficult and dangerous times. Do not take aggressive action for this will lead you into further difficulty. This may be a test of your integrity and commitment to your true principles. It is a time for non action. You may not be ready for the storm that lies ahead. Retreat, let it pass and you will be in a much better position.

63. CHI CHI

WATER *above*

FIRE *below*

Chaos has now passed and the time to prepare to be rewarded. Conduct yourself properly and without arrogance and you will benefit greatly. Keep on your toes and be mindfull that things don't slip away on you. This can be a very favourable time for you if the right principles are applied.

64. WEI CHIN

FIRE *above*

WATER *bolow*

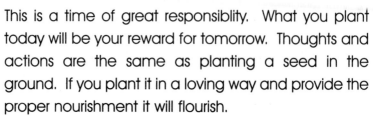

This is a time of great responsiblity. What you plant today will be your reward for tomorrow. Thoughts and actions are the same as planting a seed in the ground. If you plant it in a loving way and provide the proper nourishment it will flourish.

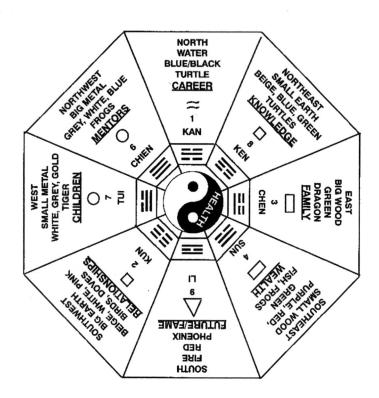

CHAPTER THREE

THE PA KUA
GRID

The Pa Kua is an octagon shaped tool that is used by Feng Shui practitioners to read energy within a space. Pa means eight and Kua means trigram and is taken from the ancient text of the I Ching. The Pa Kua is placed over the layout of a building, office, home, room or property and is used to locate areas of a space that relates to the eight areas of life. These areas are career, knowledge, family, wealth, future, relationships, children and mentors. The Pa Kua grid is an effective tool for analyzing the effects of chi flow within a space.

CAREER

Trigram: Water Direction: North

This section of a space influences your career choice. In a home it is a good area to place an office or work space. If trying to advance or encourage a career change this area should be activated by adding water such as fountains or fish tanks. Motivating pictures, diploma's or certificates are also excellent choices. Avoid using the colour red or fire features.

FUTURE

Trigram: Fire Direction: South

This sector represents your future goals and dreams. Inspirational items and objects such as trophies, ribbons, awards or travel pictures should be placed in this area. If you are not sure of your future goals or would like to activate this area place bright lights, plants or crystals in this area. Place candles, colourful mobiles and red accents in the area to activate.

MENTORS

Trigram: Heaven Direction: Northwest

The Heaven sector of the grid corresponds to helpful people and spiritual assistance. This is the best area to display statues or pictures of saints, angels, buddha or anything that is spiritual in nature for you. Mirrors, windchimes, altars or pictures of hero's are also excellent choices.

CHILDREN

Trigram: Lake Direction: West

This trigram corresponds to children and also to creativity. special projects, or anything that requires nurturing and growth. Display photographs of children, artwork and playful objects. This sector is good for a child's room, nursery or an art studio.

RELATIONSHIPS

Trigram: Earth Direction: Southwest

The earth trigram represents close relationship such as spouse, lover or partner. Statues, clay pots and other earth objects should be placed in this area. Earth tones such as beige and browns and the colour pink should be used in this sector. Relationships can be enhanced by putting things in pairs such as two candles, two photos, pictures of two people walking or two turtledoves. In a home this is an excellent choice for a master bedroom.

KNOWLEDGE

Trigram: Mountain Direction: Northeast

The trigram mountain represents an area of personal development. Books, bookcases, inspirational poetry, computers and televisons are suitable for this sector. Pictures of mountains and gentle waterfalls are also suggested in this area.

FAMILY

Trigram: Thunder Direction: East

The thunder trigram represents family, ancestors, community and friends. These are people who have great influence in your life. Family portraits, heirlooms, keepsakes, antique furniture and memorabilia should be kept in this area. Flowering plants, bright lights, crystals and mobiles will keep this area activated. This sector influences health so keep it well maintained and free from clutter.

WEALTH

Trigram: Wind Direction: Southeast

The wind trigram corresponds to money, prosperity and can also mean self-empowerment. Keep the area well lit, clear of clutter and place a live healthy plant here if you want your riches to grow. Items of value such as crystal dishes, coins or a silver tea set are effective when displayed in the wealth area. Fish tanks and tabletop fountains are considered lucky in this area.

HEALTH

The centre of the pa kua is considered to be the heart of a space. When this section is too cluttered it will block the flow of energy to the rest of the area. On the other hand if it is empty then the room is considered without a heart. Consider how a room would look if the furniture was placed against walls and the centre left empty. An area carpet, dining table and chandelier are common items for this area. A healthy living space is similar to the human body:

health begins with the heart and radiates outward.

POWER AREA

The power area of any room is the furthest corner from the door. It is the area that has the best view of the room while allowing the occupant maximum response time if someone enters the room. Use plants, flowers, fountains or crystals to activate this area.

Each aspiration is associated with a trigram of the I Ching, compass direction, element, colour, season, and symbol (see previous chapter).

The Pa Kua ideally fits over a square or rectangular space. If the area is T, U or L or odd shaped then one or more of the areas may not be included within the grid. Once the Pa Kua is properly oriented over a space it becomes a valuable tool for identifying problem areas, applying cures and encouraging the flow of positive energies. There are several ways of aligning the Pa Kua Grid over a space

FRONT DOOR ORIENTATION

This method is was devised by the Black Sect School of Feng Shui and calls the grid the Ba Gua. The grid is oriented according the the location of the front door. You always enter through either the knowledge, career or mentors area of the Ba Gua. If the door falls on the right you enter through the mentors area, if the door was in the centre you would enter through career and if the door is on the left you enter through knowledge. The wealth area will always be located in the far left corner and the relationship area is on the right etc. In the sample below note that the wealth area has a missing piece.

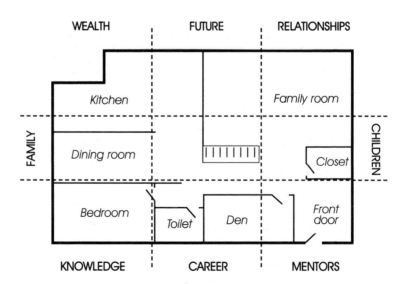

COMPASS METHOD

The compass method uses magnetic direction to orient the Pa Kua over a space. In the sample below the grid is placed with the north sector over the kitchen area so the career sector of the home is located in the kitchen area. The southeast or wealth area of the home is located over the front door as well as in the den. The den in this case would be a great place to do business. Note that the mentors area in the northwest sector is missing a piece. Compass direction can be useful when selecting property location for home or business or choosing which room is best for which function.

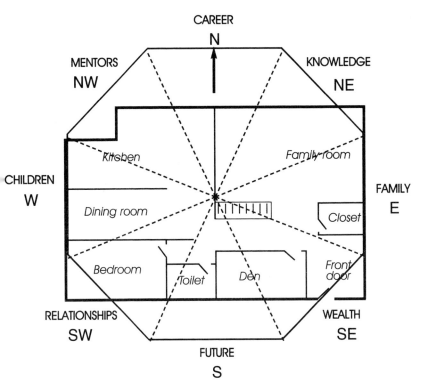

MISSING AND EXTENDED AREAS

Traditional Feng Shui believes that the home should be a square shape, but with today's designs this is not always possible. Spaces that appear to have a missing area could be foreseen as a possible problem in that area of life and on the other hand if a home has an extended area it may simple mean that there may be an abundance in that area of life. If, for example, the wealth area is missing then the occupants may have difficulty accumulating money. However, if the area is extended the occupants may be blessed with an abundance of wealth. When possible fill in the missing area with energy from lights, plants, birdbaths or fountains. Try to create the illusion that the area is squared off. That can be done by using shrubs lights or rocks.

KUA
YOUR MOST FAVOURABLE COMPASS DIRECTION

To determine the most auspicious direction for your front door, your bed or your favourite chair, you must first determine which direction corresponds with your year of birth. This number is often referred to as your Kua number. Refer to the appendices section of this book.

The kua number is based on the lunar calender so if your birth month falls on January or early February use the previous year to determine your kua. The number for females and male differ so be sure to look under the proper category. There are a number of advanced formulas to help determine personal best and worst directions as well as good and bad front door directions, however for a beginner it is best to stay with a simple approach. Note that the kua number is only for determining best sitting or facing directions as well as the best facing direction for your bed or front door. When it is not possible to sit or face in your personal best direction add the colour of the element associated with your best direction to bridge the gap. As this may sound a little confusing at first it is best use the easy reference chart for front door directions in the appendices section of this book.

The chart can also be used to determine the best facing direction for your bed. The facing direction of the bed is determined according to where your head points when you lie in bed.

CHAPTER FOUR

THE FIVE ELEMENTS

The Five-Element Theory is an elegant system developed by the Taoists as a way of understanding the interacting phases of chi energy. The five elements represent everything in the universe that is visible and invisible. Based on observation, the Chinese concluded that the entire universe is based on cycles and rhythms of yin and yang chi energy affecting each other in a play of creation, reduction and domination. Cycles in our world begin with each day with the sun rising in the east and setting in the west. The year begins with the cold winter giving way to the spring then summer followed by the fall and then winter again.

Like yin/yang and chi, the Five Element Theory is an important principle of good Feng Shui. The elements are Wood, Fire, Earth, Metal and Water. In their productive cycle each of the elements gives way to the other. Wood is the fuel for fire, which burns to earth, and in turn earth produces metals and metal attracts and holds water and water gives life to wood. The creative cycle of the elements represents harmony and balance. When the elements are off balance the dominant or reduction cycle is used to make adjustments.

The elements are associated with compass direction, colours, shapes, seasons, feelings and characteristics. Landscapes, buildings, rooms, doors and people can be characterized by the five elements. Depending on the purpose of a room the five elemental energies can be used to activate, enhance or balance any space. If, for example, relaxation is what is desired for a bedroom add earth energy and if energy is needed in the family room then add fire or wood.

The elements themselves such as wood in the form of plants, water as in a fountain or earth in the form of a clay pot are ideal ways to add elements but if this is not possible add the element colour. Each element has it's own shape or pattern and this too can be used to introduce it's energy into a space.

WOOD

COLOUR	*Green*
DIRECTION	*East*
SEASON	*Spring*
TIME OF DAY	*Dawn*
SHAPE	*Rectangle*
SYMBOL	*Dragon*
CHARACTERISTIC	*Nourishment, upward growth, creativity, renewal, change, ideas*
FEELINGS	*Fresh, happy, active, hope, adventurous*
BUILDINGS	*Tall, rectangular, skyscrapers, towers, healing centers, restaurants and hospitals*
ROOMS	*Children's bedrooms, kitchens, dining rooms and treatment rooms.*
OBJECTS	*Trees, plants, flowers, wooden frames, books, newspapers, organic fibers such as linen or cotton*

Tall rectangular skyscrapers represent the wood element.

FIRE

COLOUR   *Red and Purple*
DIRECTION   *South*
SEASON   *Summer*
TIME OF DAY   *High noon*
SHAPE   *Triangle*
SYMBOL   *Phoenix*
CHARACTERISTIC   *Action, activity, agitation and power*
FEELINGS   *Enthusiasm, hot, energy and excitement*
BUILDINGS   *Pointed and angled roofs, churches,
casinos, dance-halls, libraries, schools,
vet clinics and high fashion industry*
ROOMS   *Game rooms and ceremonial rooms*
OBJECTS   *Candles, light bulbs and fire*

A Church with a triangular shaped roof is a fire building.

EARTH

COLOUR	*Terra cotta and all earth tones.*
DIRECTION	*Centre and southwest*
SEASON	*Late summer*
TIME OF DAY	*Mid afternoon*
SHAPE	*Square*
SYMBOL	*Earth*
CHARACTERISTIC	*Solid, even, stable and grounded*
FEELINGS	*Comfortable, safe and secure*
BUILDINGS	*Low, square, brick and concrete, Hospitals, courthouses, jails, retirement homes and storage units.*
ROOMS	*Sitting rooms, storage rooms, garages and conservatories*
OBJECTS	*Bricks, clay, concrete, sand and rocks*

These low, square buildings represent the earth element.

METAL

COLOUR	*White, silver, grey and gold*
DIRECTION	*West*
SEASON	*Autumn*
TIME OF DAY	*Dawn*
SHAPE	*Round, oval or domed*
SYMBOL	*White tiger*
CHARACTERISTIC.	*Sharp, refined and precise.*
FEELINGS	*Focused, clear and moral*
BUILDINGS	*Domed roofs, reflective buildings, financial institutions, observatries hardware, jewelers and computer stores,*
ROOMS	*Kitchens, bathrooms and workshops*
OBJECTS	*Metal, gold and steel coins, medals, mirrors, wires and wind chimes*

This observatory's domed roof is a metal shaped.

WATER

COLOUR	*Blue and black*
DIRECTION	*North*
SEASON	*Winter*
TIME OF DAY	*Midnight*
SHAPE	*Undulating*
SYMBOL	*Turtle*
CHARACTERISTIC	*Yielding, transmission of ideas, comfortable, easy and social interaction*
FEELINGS	*Relaxed, easy going and clear thinking*
BUILDINGS	*Glass, nurseries, travel agencies, aquariums and broadcasting*
ROOMS	*Laundry, bathrooms, and treatment rooms*
OBJECTS	*Fish bowls, fountains, glass & plastics*

A nursery with a water shaped roof.

THE FIVE ELEMENT CYCLES

CYCLE OF CREATION

Water grows and nourishes wood
Wood creates and feeds fire
Fire burns and makes earth
Earth particles make metal
Metal attracts and holds water

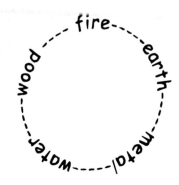

THE CYCLE OF REDUCTION

Water reduces metal by rusting
Metal reduces earth by condensing
Earth smothers fire
Fire burns and consumes wood
Wood absorbs water

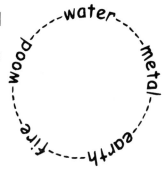

THE CYCLE OF DOMINATION

Earth stops water
Water puts out fire
Fire melts metal
Metal chops wood
Wood consumes earth

CHAPTER FIVE

CURES AND TIPS

CURES

LIGHT

The amount of light in your surroundings has a profound affect on health and emotions. Lack of sunlight can create feelings of depression whereas sunlight energizes and uplifts.

* Increase lighting by replacing bulbs with higher wattage or use full spectrum bulbs.

* Lamps and spotlights can be used to highlight objects and plants creating a different dimension.

* Diversion can be created by pointing a lamp or spotlight over a shiny object on a table or counter.

* Crystal prisms hung in front of a window disperse white light as a rainbow of colours.

* Position a mirror across from a window to bring more light into a room.

COLOUR

Studies from around the world indicate that colours directly affect they way we feel. In a recent study, prison cells painted bubble gum pink resulted in less agitated prisoners. Red is a high energy colour that can be used to elevate moods and attract attention such as with stop signs or traffic lights. Colour is used to create a desired effect in a room.

* When selecting colours use the creative cycle of tho five elements to create balance. Wood (green) to fire (red, pink, peach) to earth (brown, beige, yellow) to metal (white, gray or reflective) to water (blue, navy or black). By using tints and tones of the primary colours, harmony and balance can easily be achieved. A colour scheme for a living room may look like this:

1. Green carpet, peach walls and beige ceiling (wood-fire-earth)
2. Red carpet, beige walls and white ceiling (fire-earth-metal)
3. Silver carpet, blue walls and green ceiling (metal-water-wood)

To achieve perfect harmony accent the room with the missing elements:

1. Gray and black accents (metal and water)
2. Blue or black and green (water and wood)
3. Red and brown (fire and earth)

SOUND

By definition sound is a vibration that causes a sensation in the ear experienced as noise or sound depending on the recipient's interpretation. A teenager's music may be noise to an adult whereas they would find an adult's music annoying. Sound is an important part of Feng Shui and should be included as part of a harmonious environment in your home. Whether you are living alone or with a large family the introduction of sound can encourage positive energy in any space.

* Windchimes create a gentle tinkling sound when the wind brushes against them. Hang a windchime outside a door or close to a window. Hollow tubes on metal windchimes are the most auspicious.

* Place leafy plants near slightly open windows to encourage the rustling of the leaves.

* Use automatic timers to turn music on at regular intervals.

* Place a bird bath or bird house outside windows to attract singing birds.

SMELL

The nose is never asleep. When the sense of smell meets freshly baked bread or cotton candy our memory evokes past experiences like Mom's home baking or the trip to the Fair. With the popularity of aroma-therapy dozens of fragrances and scents can be introduced into an environmont to create a number of desired effects. There are scents that can relax, uplift and relieve stress. All of these can be introduced by incenses, candles, sprays, oils and small ceramic pots. For samples see page 125.

LIFE

Life can be added to a home in the form of animals or plants. Studies have proven that caring for a plant or pet can be both rewarding and healthy.

*Domestic pets such as birds, cats and dogs add life to a home. They can certainly benefit people living alone such as senior citizens.

* Birdhouses and baths can be placed outside the window to attract wild and cheerful birds.

* Various types of bushes, flowers or trees can be used to attract colourful butterflies

* Chinese money plant or jade is considered lucky, especially in the wealth area.

* Gold fish in a fish bowl can double your luck. Gold and red fish symbolize money and wealth. Nine fish that include one black and eight gold is very lucky.

* Plants and flowers help to soften the effects of sharp edges in a room.

* Live plants serve to uplift energy and add life to a room.

* Cut flowers add colour and should be replaced when wilted or dying.

* Dried flowers do not add life to a room although synthetic flowers and plants are acceptable.

* Avoid too many prickly cactus or other desert plants.

MOVEMENT

Movement is an ideal way to introduce life into a still area. Movement summons attention and is good as a distraction.

* Wind-sensitive objects include: flags, banners, mobiles, windmills and fans and they are ideal for creating movement.

WATER

Water is considered to be very lucky in Feng Shui. Life on earth cannot be sustained without it. Having this element present in a home can encourage and uplift energy. Water represents wealth and prosperity in traditional Feng Shui.

* Tabletop fountains, aquariums and fish bowls are excellent ways of bringing water into a home.

* Trickling sounds of indoor water fountain or aquarium is soothing and relaxing.

* Water fountains are visually pleasing, uplifting and add moisture to the air.

MIRRORS

Mirrors are great cures in Feng Shui. They can be used for many different purposes including expanding a space, bringing in light, making a space disappear and reflecting a beautiful scene.

* Do not hang a mirror in a position where it cuts off people's heads.

* Place mirrors across from a dining area to double the quantity of food.

* Placing a mirror in a confined area can make it appear larger, such as the inside of an elevator.

* Placing a mirror on a bathroom door can make it disappear.

* Avoid tiled mirrors on walls as they break up your image.

* Replace all cracked or chipped mirrors.

* When a room has only one window, hang a mirror directly across from it and it will appear like there are two windows in the room.

SYMBOLS & STATUES

Symbols and statues can be wonderful Feng Shui cures.

* Framed pictures of saints, angels or spirit guides can be spiritually uplifting in any area of the home, especially in the Mentor area.

* Outdoor heavy statues such as lions and gargoyles can be used to symbolically guard the home against intruders. It is best to display less aggressive animals indoors.

* Use personal symbols and objects that represent meaning to you in any area to enhance energy.

TIPS

PATHWAYS

* Pathways leading to a home should be kept in good condition.

* Pot holes, cracks and a broken sidewalks are an indication of a life in disrepair. Repairing the main roads and sidewalks is the responsibility of the local municipalities so group together neighbours and voice your concern.

* First impressions are the most important so keep driveway and pathways in good repair.

* Plant flowers and plants alongside the pathway leading to the front door.

* Straight and narrow pathways should be curved or widened. This can easily be done by intermitently adding shrubs and flowers along the sides.

* Front doors should be visible and welcoming. If the entrance cannot be seen from the driveway or pathway add bright lights, wind chimes or position a mirror so that the door can be seen from the driveway.

FRONT ENTRANCES

The front entrance of a home is an indication of what lies inside. It reflects how the occupants feel about themselves.

* The front door is the mouth of chi and should be kept in good repair, ensure that there is no peeling paint or cracks in the door.

* The door should be in proper proportion to the size of the home. Large double doors are well suited to large homes where a single well-manicured door looks lovely on a smaller home.

* Townhouse or apartment doors can be distinguished from the others by hanging plants, door ornaments or by placing a doormat on the threshold.

* Doors should open wide just as a welcoming embrace. When doors don't open completely it gives the impression of something to hide.

* When a front door opens and faces another door or

window the energy is said to flow in one door and out the other. Create diversions that will pull the energy towards the main gathering area of the home.

STAIRWAYS

* When the front door opens to face the stairs the occupants of the home may want to spend most of their time upstairs. Place a plant, heavy object or mirror to direct the chi energy towards the main area of the home.

* Stairs with open backs are inauspicious. If they cannot be covered put plants or heavy objects under the staircase.

* Spiral staircases can be compared to a corkscrew that drills and burrows into the space. Avoid a staircase in the middle of a home as it pierces the heart or the centre of the home. Do not use red carpeting on spiral stairs. The best location for these types of stairs is in the back corners of homes.

* Curved or gently winding staircases are the most auspicious.

* Hang pictures or mirrors on the walls of long narrow staircases.

WINDOWS

* Windows are considered the eyes of a home and

should be kept in good repair.

* Replace all broken or cracked windows and keep them clean and free of clutter.

* When a brick wall is seen from the window, cover with an appropriate window dressing or hang planters or crystals to block the view.

CEILINGS

Ceilings are the sky of space and should be painted in a light airy color.

* When the ceiling is too high, using a darker shade can bring it down.

* Beams on low ceilings create an oppressive feeling and should be as inconspicuous as possible. Paint them the same color as the ceiling, hang crystals or wind sensitive objects.

* Do not place a sofa, bed or chair under a beam.

* Distract away from ceiling beams by placing shiny objects or brighter lights at eye level.

BATHROOMS

The bathroom door should always be kept closed, especially if the bathroom is located close to an entrance or near a gathering area. The toilet seat should be kept down at all times as it is believed that all the chi energy will be flushed away down the drains.

* Hang a crystal prism from the window to encourage positive energy.

* Keep a small fresh plant in the washroom and avoid stale pot pourri and dried flowers.

* When the bathroom door faces a main seating or sleeping area paint it the same colour as the wall, keep door closed and put up pictures or place heavy objects on the side of the door to create a diversion.

* When space permits place a screen or wall separating the toilet from the bathtub.

* Bright lighting and mirrors are auspicious in bathrooms.

* White, green, blue or beige are good colours for bathroom walls.

KITCHEN

* Kitchens or refridgerators that are visible from the front door may cause overeating. Keep the lights closed when not in use. Place a planter on the side of the kitchen door or hang a crystal between the two doors to create a diversion.

* The stove is the most important part of the kitchen and should be kept clean and in good repair. Be sure all of the elements are in working order.

* If the cook's back faces the door while cooking a

mirror should be placed over the stove so that the kitchen door can be seen.

* Kitchen areas should be well-lit and cheerful. Auspicious colours for sinks are metal, black or white.

* Avoid the colour red for a sink. Good colours for a kitchen are white, green, blue or cream.

DINING ROOM

* Oval or round tables are best as they allow the chi to flow all around.

* Tables should be brightly lit by a ceiling light or chandelier centered over the table.

* Avoid beams over the table.

* Table should be the centre of focus and in the middle of the room.

* Mirror reflecting the table is auspicious as it doubles the food.

* Good colours for the dining area are white, green and orange.

LIVING ROOM/GATHERING AREA

* Depending on the main use of the living area it should be well-lit and relaxing.

* Sofas and chairs should be arranged to face each other.

* Allow sufficient room around each piece of furni-

ture for easy movement.

* Sofas and chairs should have their backs to the wall.

* Keep corners free of clutter.

* The television should never be the center of attraction in a gathering area. Never put the television in the power area of the room (the area of a room that is the furthest from the door and has the clearest view of the entire room.)

* The power area of the living room should be reserved for self-empowerment or study. A comfortable chair with a reading table and lamp is best in this area.

BEDROOMS

* Bedrooms are for rest and relaxation, therefore exercise machines, televisions and ironing boards should be avoided. When the last thing you see before going to bed is related to work you may cause difficulty falling asleep.

* Headboards should be well-fastened and against a solid wall.

* Position beds so that there is a clear view of the room's entrance.

* High-energy colours such as red should be avoided on walls and ceilings.

* Mirrors on the ceiling are not appropriate for a bed-

room and can cause anxious restless feelings.

* Never position a mirror across from a bed. Your energy level when you first awake or when you go to sleep is low and is reflected back to you in the mirror.

* When encouraging or improving a relationship keep both sides of the bed open. Do not push one side against the wall.

* Keep the room free of clutter. Overstuffed closets and drawers can make you feel restless and fatigued. Remove all items and objects from under your bed as they also affect you.

* Rooms overtop the garage are not auspicious for a bedroom. If this cannot be helped be sure the garage is free of clutter and kept clean and dry.

* Pictures of action scenes or turbulent storms should be avoided in a bedroom.

* Place sachets of relaxing scents in pillowcases.

* Ideal colours for the bedroom are blue, green, beige and violet.

TIPS FOR BUYING OR BUILDING A HOME

* *Research* history of the home. Who were the previous owners? Why did they sell? What occupied the land before the home was built?

* *Vegetation* around the home will give you an indication of the home to the environment. Are the large

trees diseased or damaged? What types of trees, shrubs and flowers surround the home? Some trees attract butterflies while others attract annoying insects.

* *Check Compass direction* and determine what sides of the home the sun hits when it rises and sets. Will the sun shine on the garden? Is your home protected from the cold damaging winds? Is the home *higher* than others? If a home is surrounded by other homes, large buildings hovering over it, the occupants may feel inferior.

* Does the *driveway slope* down or is it elevated? A driveway that slopes down may be lead to flooding of the basement. It is always best to climb up to your home rather than to step down.

* Is there a body of *water* nearby and if so what life does it support? Stagnant water often contains chemicals that kill vegetation and attract unappealing insect life.

* Check *below ground.* If you are purchasing a lot you may want to *check below ground level* for abnormalities such as a clay bottom or high water table that could make building a home unsuitable or costly.

* Check for *high voltage generators* or *hydro lines* that emit electromagnetic waves. Be sure that they

are a safe distance from the home or lot.

Avoid a home that is located across from a *ceme-tery, factory or repair shop.*

HOME OFFICES OR WORK AREAS

* Home-based offices are best located close to the front or back door to keep customers from entering the main areas of your home.

* Position desks and chairs with back to a solid wall.

* Desks are best located facing the entrance to the room and in the furthest space away from the door.

* When the desk faces a window, position a mirror in front of you so that the room's entrance can be seen when seated.

* Concave mirror can be easily placed on top of the monitor.

* Keep your work area free of paperwork and clutter. Discard or remove all excess paperwork that is not regularly used or needed.

* Store files in closed boxes or file cabinets and keep bills out of sight.

* Work area should be well-lit and inspiring. Be sure that the light is not causing shadows over your work area. Dim lights and shadows cause eyestrain and fatigue.

GENERAL TIPS

* Blank walls in a home say nothing. Walls are great for communicating messages of relaxation and inspiration.

* Use the Pa Kua as a guide and hang decorative objects, pictures, photos and certificates on all walls where appropriate. Carefully select what you display in the children's room as they are easily influenced by the images they look at regularly.

* Remove dead or dying plants from your home.

* When decorating keep in mind the purpose of the room, the creative cycles of the elements and yin and yang balance.

* All rooms should have all of the five elements represented and can be by way of element, colour, object or shape.

* Plants can be used too fill empty spaces and add life.

* Avoid dried flowers they are devoid of life and create stale energy.

* Synthetic flowers are fine as they have been artistically created.

CHAPTER SIX

CASE STUDIES

CASE FILE #1

CLIENT

Tony, a 32-year-old single man, works as a warehouse manager for a Wholesale Distribution Company. His shift begins at 4 in the afternoon and ends at 1:30am. He shares a large condo with his retired parents. His home is laid out in such a way that he occupies one end of the condo containing one large bedroom, a smaller room and a four-piece bathroom.

CONCERN
- Problems falling asleep at night
- Lack of energy during the day
- Has no social life

OBSERVATION
- The headboard of his bed is located directly under a beam.
- The bed is positioned in such a way that when he lies down his feet line up with the bedroom door.
- Clutter is found in every corner of his room, under his bed and in his closet.

- A picture of a high-speed race depicting an airborne car that struck a wall is located on the wall directly across from his bed. The other walls are all blank.
- His computer workstation is located in his bedroom and occupies the entire relationship area.
- There are numerous wires sticking out from his computer, printer, fax machine and video game.
- Boxes, books and CDs are scattered on the desk and on the floor. Garbage is piled high in the corner next to the desk. The aroma from two ashtrays, filled to the brim with butts, permeates the entire room.
- The spare room is used as a storage area for old clothes, boxes of books and odds and ends.

CURES

Beams above the head create an oppressive energy that can create an un-restful feeling.
- Relocate the bed to the opposite side of the wall.
- Feet pointing almost directly out the door can cause feelings of exposure and uneasiness. Moving the bed to the opposite wall will solve this problem.
- Move the mirrored dresser across the bed and over for a full view of the bedroom entrance.

- Clutter creates stale energy in a room and can create fatigue. Remove all of the excess clutter from the room. Pack up all items that are unused and unwanted and give them to charity or store them away in labeled boxes.

- The picture of the crashing racecar does not create a comforting restful feeling. Relocate the picture to another room.

- Remove the computer and electronic equipment out of the relationship area of the room and relocate into the smaller room next door. This smaller room can serve as a den and entertainment center. Relocate the large garbage bin into the den area.

- Blank walls in the relationship area indicate that there is nothing going on. Hang pictures of people in groups or in pairs. Items or objects in pairs, such as two candles, two statues, two cars or two birds will also work.

- Purchase plug-in aroma decanter. Lavender, vanilla or patchouli infuse relaxation.

Several weeks after the consultation Tony advised me that he was sleeping much better and that his energy level was improving. As a result of relocating the computer and electronic equipment into the smaller room he felt motivated in the morning and enjoyed going into his den. He also felt energetic enough to go out with some of his friends after work. On one of the outings three different women approached him. Two of the girls are now fighting over Tony and he wonders if perhaps he Feng Shui'd his room a little too much.

CASE FILE #2

CLIENT

Annabelle is a single, 42-year-old woman who has been living on her own for 5 years and lives in a spacious one bedroom apartment. She enjoys her full-time position as a travel agent in a large downtown office.

CONCERN

Feels down and tired most of the time
● Would like to socialize more often
● Is interested in meeting a man and cultivating a
● meaningful relationship.

OBSERVATION
● Entire apartment is extremely tidy and appears free of clutter.

- Apartment is decorated in muted earth tones of beige browns and pale yellow.
- Kitchen is green and beige and has a small round table with a single decorative place mat. The
- table can seat two but she has removed a chair and is left with a single seat.
- Living-room furniture is brown, bulky and bottom heavy.
- A large dried flower arrangement on her dining room table and two bouquets of dried roses in her bedroom.
- Walls in the living room are adorned with several pieces of expensive artwork depicting old European village scenes.
- Apartment is carpeted in a plush taupe color.
- Window dressing is beige and made of thick heavy material with square patterns.
- Bedroom is painted in soft blue with pink accents.
- One side of the bed is pushed against the wall and she only has one end table with one lamp
- Closets are filled to the brim with clothing and shoes and drawers are also completely stuffed.
- The walls in the bedroom are blank with the exception of a glamorous photo of herself.

CURES

Annabelle feels down and tired all of the time for many reasons. Firstly of all the colours in her living-room, where she spends most of her time, consist of dark, earth tones. These colours are great for comfort and security but when used in the extreme tend to induce relaxation and lack of motivation. The furniture is bulky, bottom heavy and makes the room feel crowded and blocked in. The artwork of the old street scenes creates a feeling of loneliness and antiquity. The "earth" feeling in the living-room makes Annabelle wants to stay at home and relax. The indicators in the kitchen and the bedroom are that of a single woman who lives alone. One place setting, one chair and one single photo all reinforce loneliness, whereas pairs or things in twos suggest company. To increase energy and attract a relationship apply these cures:

- Remove one of the square bulky chairs and relocate to the bedroom.
- Add two lamps with full spectrum lighting in the living room.
- Change the window dressing to semi-see-through veil type material. Keep the window slightly open so that the curtains will sway when brushed by a breeze.

- Purchase two bright red pillows for the sofa.
  Place a crystal candy dish filled with mints on the coffee table.
- Remove all dried flower arrangements and replace with live plants.
- Keep a bouquet of colourful fresh flowers on the dining room table.
- Add another chair and place mat to the kitchen table.
- Move bed away from the wall and add another end table and lamp.
- Put up pictures of things in pairs; two lovers, two birds, two flowers.
- Remove some clothing from the closets to make room for guests.

In a follow up phone call, Annabelle was happy to advise me that she is now seeing a man who was introduced to her through a co-worker. In a casual conversation during a lunch break, Annabelle mentioned the Feng Shui consultation. A few days later one of the girls introduced her to a friend who was instantly attracted to her.

CASE FILE #3

CLIENT

Mrs. Smith is 39 year-old and married with two children, an 8-year-old girl and a 10-year-old boy. Her husband works as an account executive for a large firm and she stays at home with the children. They recently purchased a new 4-bedroom home in the suburbs. Since purchasing the home, Mrs. Smith has noticed that her relationship with her husband has become stressed and that her children have become difficult to handle. She feels that perhaps there is bad energy in the home.

CONCERN

- Mr. Smith is spending more and more time away from home.
- The children's attention span is very low and her oldest boy has lost interest in sports and is not motivated.
- Although their financial situation is very comfortable they have difficulty holding on to their money.

OBSERVATION

- A large tree sits directly facing the front door.
- The front door ines up directly with the back door.

- A large portion of the wealth area of the home is missing and there is a compost heap replacing the area on the outside.
- There are no pictures of Mr. & Mrs. Smith anywhere in the home.
- Entrance of room cannot be seen from bed.
- The 10-year-old boy's bedroom is painted white and the walls are blank.
- The kitchen, where the family spends most of their time, has a large window that faces a playground.

CURES

The Smith's were doing fine until they moved into their new home so the problem seems to stem from the arrangement of the space they occupy. To create harmony and strengthen relationships the living space must first be in harmony with the occupants. I suggested the following cures:

- Suspend a birdhouse from the tree that faces the front door. This will attract birds, defuse negative energy and create movement and life.
- Hang a windchime outside the front door. The sound and the movement create positive energy that begins at the front door.
- Place a plant between the front and the back

door to stop the energy from flowing in one door and out the other.

- Create a window covering for the kitchen window that covers the bottom half only. This will mask the playground from the children while seated at the kitchen table.

- Put a plant in front of the corner that protrudes from the missing wealth area to diffuse the cutting energy caused by the poison arrow.

- Relocate the compost from the outside of the wealth area to the side of the garage or to a discreet area in the back yard. Place shrubs and plants to square off the outside of the house.

- Place a small table-top fountain in the wealth corner beside the plant. The sound from the fountain will calm, soothe and create a positive atmosphere.

- Hang personal photos in the dining room and in particular in all of the relationship areas of the home, especially the bedroom.

- Reposition the bed in the master bedroom so that there is a full view of the entrance to the room.

- For motivation of the 10-year-old boy, place trophies or awards on the dresser that face his bed so that he can look at them and feel proud. The walls should be filled with inspirational motivating pictures of favourite sports figures or of those he looks up to.

One of the first cures that Mrs. Smith applied was the table-top fountain. She noticed her children calmed down each time that the fountain was turned on. Later the same week her husband announced that he signed on a huge client which meant an immediate increase in pay.

CASE FILE #4

CLIENT
Kelly, 28, is single and lives in a small town-house with her dog and two cats. She works full-time at a man-ufacturing plant and part- time as a therapist.

CONCERN
- Career change
  Increase social activity
- Create a nurturing and relaxing atmosphere at home
- Would like to travel more often

OBSERVATION
- Pathway leding to house is narrow and straight.

- Front entrance is located in the career section. The entrance-way is narrow and there is an open door-
- way immediately to the right with a step staircase leading to the basement.
- The hallway is painted in a bright fuchsia colour.
- Four low, dark-brown beams are located on the ceiling directly above the living room seating area.
- The living room is decorated with blue walls, blue carpeting and black, blue and purple furniture.

CURES

Kelly finds her full-time job stressful and unfulfilling. The high noise level of the machines makes her feel nervous and stressed. She has difficulty unwinding and relaxing when she returns home from work. She would like to have people over and socialize but always feels like going out or being somewhere else. She feels that traveling is the answer but can not afford to do so unless she brings in more money. She enjoys her work as a therapist and would rather work at that than her present job at the plant. Most of Kelly's frustrations are related to the energy created by the some of the structural detail and the decor of her home. To create balance and harmony in the home I suggest the following:

- Create a curved pathway by adding a few planters filled with colourful flowers.
- Place windchimes at the entrance to the home.
- For safety , put up a door on the entrance into the basement and hang a full length mirror.
- Repaint the entrance hallway a light green colour.
- Plug in a lemon/lime scented defuser in hallway.
- Remove oppressive energy from ceiling beams by painting them white, same as ceiling colour.
- Place a crystal candy dish on the coffee table and fill with mints.
- Display shiny objects on the coffee table such as gold or silver candle holders.
- Purchase a tabletop water fountain and place next to the living room sliding door. Attach an automatic timer so that it turns on at regular intervals.
- Add green plants to the living room.

Kelly was so pleased with the changes that she made to her home that she held a dinner party and invited a few neighbours and friends. It turned out that one of her neighbours owned a natural health clinic and offered Kelly a full time job that offered more pay.

CASE FILE #5

CLIENT

Mrs. Jones, 40, is married with two grown children. For the past two years she has been unemployed, due to downsizing. She feels fatigued most of the time and is certain that it has something to do with her home.

CONCERN

- Can't sleep nights
- Wants to find a job
- Would like to feel good in her home

OBSERVATION

- Mrs. Jones home is filled with clutter. Magazines, boxes, broken and mended antiques are in every area of the house, including the basement.
- In the centre of the living-room there is a large cream-coloured, oval rug with a huge, dark stain in the middle.
- Every table, counter and shelf is filled with old collectable, antique trinkets and ornaments, most of which are damaged.
- The mirrored dresser in the master bedroom faces the bed.
- Next to the dresser is a laundry basket over-filled

with soiled laundry.

- An exercise bike occupies the right-hand side of the bed.

CURES

Mrs. Jones has difficulty sleeping at nights and in turn cannot function during the day. What she sees at night before she goes to sleep affects her sleep. She lacks the enthusiasm and motivation that is needed to go out and look for a job. She constantly feels confused, tired and frustrated. When she goes out, all she thinks about is things she needs to do at home. I suggested the following cures:

- Discard all old magazines, newspapers and books sitting in boxes.
- Clear out the basement and sell, give away or repair all of the antique furniture.
- Either have the stain on the oval carpeting professionally cleaned or discard of the carpet entirely.
- Remove all of the damaged ornaments from the tables and counters and seal, label and store in boxes.
- Rearrange the mirrored dresser so it does not face the bed.
- Replace the open laundry basket with a covered

hamper to hide the soiled clothing.

● Remove the exercise bike from the room and relocate to the spare room or basement.

In a follow-up conversation with Mrs Jones she was happy to report that her energy level increased substantially after clearing away most of the clutter and applying the cures. With the help of her husband she filled her van with all of the antiques and trinkets from her home and began selling them at a local flea market. As a result she started her own antique business and is currently very happy.

CASE FILE #6

CLIENT

Marybeth is a 24-year-old university student and is studying to be an architect. She lives at home with her parents and younger brother. Marybeth is extremely motivated and has always been an honour student. Her father John is a lawyer and her mother, Catherine is a homemaker. John and Catherine decided to give her the use of John's den which is located in a private area towards the back of the house. Marybeth's parents thought that this would help her with studies in her last year of university.

CONCERN

- Marybeth has not been able to concentrate on her studies since moving into the den
- She is going out to party more often than normal
- There has been growing conflict between mother and daughter for no apparent reason

OBSERVATION

- The wall- to- wall bookshelf in the den is filled with law books and files.
- There are boxes piled against the wall containing files and paperwork.
- The large desk is made of expensive mahogany
- wood in perfect condition.
- There are no windows in the room.
- The room is very quiet and stuffy.
- The chair is large and made of soft red leather framed with gold trim.
- There is a huge painting of "The battle of Gettysburg" on the wall in front of the desk. The painting depicts men on horses with guns shooting at each other. A lamp sits overtop the painting highlighting all the details.

CURES

Marybeth's recent actions are directly related to the

den. The room is private and well designed but she does not feel comfortable doing her work in that room. The furniture is very thick and large and is made for an executive. The energy of the room is refined, stuffy and silent. If at all possible Marybeth should return to her own room to study. She is most comfortable with a smaller desk and familiar sur-roundings. If this is not possible then I suggested the following cures:

- Remove the painting from the wall in front of the desk and replace it with a nature scene (water and mountains).
- Re-locate all the boxes on the floor into another room.
- Replace the low wattage lamp with a full spec-trum light.
- Place a halogen lamp in the corner of the room to uplift the energy in the room.
- Put a small fish bowl with three gold fish on the small counter across from the desk.
- Plug in a citrus decanter to infuse energy.

In a follow up phone call Marybeth advised me that her parents made changes to the den and as a result she spends more time studying. They replaced the "battle" painting with a nature scene, removed most of the boxes and added a small aquarium to the room. She finds the energy of the room uplifting and brighter.

CASE FILE #7

CLIENT

Carl, a 32- year-old entrepreneur is a consultant for computer software. He is single and lives alone. When he is not with customers he works out of his small two bedroom home. He is happy with his career choice and has plenty of friends that give him support.

CONCERN

- Increase wealth
- Re-decorate his office
- Control the flow of visitors during the day
- Attract a relationship

OBSERVATION

- The office is located in the Mentor area and extends out from the home. The space has it's own entrance to the side of the front door.
  The office walls are beige and the flooring is dark brown.

- Along with the regular computer equipment, the office contains a very large, comfortable black leather sofa.
- The bedroom is located in the family area of the home and has very little furniture
- One side of the bed is pushed against the wall. The walls are white and blank.

CURES

Carl keeps his home clutter-free. The furniture is well-made but sparse. Most of his decorating efforts have gone into the office in the front of the house. The office is warm and comfortable which explains why he has so many guests visiting. With family and friends constantly dropping in Carl finds it difficult to do his work. Carl is willing to make changes in his home that can help increase business and attract a meaningful relationship.

I suggested the following cures:

- Relocate the office to the bedroom in the north east corner of the home. Paint the room light blue. Add a plant in each corner.
- Arrange the desk to face the view in the backyard.
- Attach a small mirror on the computer screen in order to clearly see the entrance to the room.

- Remove the sofa from the office and relocate to the living room.
- Turn the old office into a game room with a dart-board, card table etc.
- In bedroom, move bed away from wall and add end tables and lamps on both sides.
- Paint the room light green.
- Put up pictures of couples and things in pairs.
- Place a plant in the furthest right corner of the room.

I contacted Carl to follow up on his progress and was pleased to discover that he had indeed made all of the changes. He has been getting con-tracts from large companies and is doing well in his business. His friends and relatives still come over to visit but the difference is that they hang out in the "Game Room" leaving Carl in the privacy of his own office. He has since met a girlfriend that is now help-ing him with his business.

CHAPTER SEVEN

SEVEN STEP FENG SHUI

Now you can Feng Shui your own home or office space simply by following this step by step process. As you go through these steps refer back to sections of the book that are being referred to. There are plenty of charts and references that will help guide you to the right choices. In many cases you will come up with ideas of your own that will work just as well as those suggested in this book. Don't worry if it takes you a while to finally click into the flow of things as this is normal. Feng Shui is not something you can learn in a day, month or year. It takes most masters a lifetime of study to really understand all the principles of Feng Shui. With these seven steps you can now begin the process of putting your life back into balance a step at a time.

1. EDUCATE YOURSELF

The first step is to educate yourself on Feng Shui, the art of placement. Now that you have read this far, you have begun the process of understanding. Feng Shui is a very complex system and because there are so many views on the subject it can seem confusing to the beginner.

· Read many books on Feng Shui. Check the the recommended reading section for suggestions.

· Make an effort to attend regular workshops and seminars on the subject.

· Subscribe to magazines and newsletters to keep yourself updated.

Test your knowledge

1.   Feng Shui is an ancient art that began in China around 618 AD. Give examples of how it can help in today's modern world?

2.   Name the Five Energies, their associated colours, shape and characteristics.

3. What element colour commands attention? What element colour helps promote relaxation.?

5. If there were too much of the fire element in a room what element would you add to reduce its effect?

6. How can compass direction help create a balanced space?

7. What colours and shapes would you find dominating a yin space?

2. CLARIFY YOUR GOALS
Identify your goals and concerns by answering these questions.

On a scale of 0-6 rate areas of your life.
0 - non existent 1 - bad 2 - not good
3 - average 4 - not bad 5 - good
6 - excellent

For your residence answer question a) and for work spaces refer to b)

MENTORS/HELPFUL PEOPLE
1.a) I always have the help of others when I need it.
 b) same as above

KNOWLEDGE
2. a) I make an effort to learn something new every day.
 b) same as above

CAREER

3. a) I am happy with my present career choice.

b) My job is satisfying, rewarding and fulfilling

CHILDREN/CREATIVITY

4. a) I am happy with my children's development and/or I am expressing my creativity to it's fullest
   b) I am expressing my creativity and developing new projects and ideas.

PERSONAL RELATIONSHIP

5. a) My love life is happy and fulfilling.
   b) I have a good relationship with my partner/ customers.

FAMILY

6. a) I have a good relationship with my family, friends and community.
   b) I get along with my co-workers, business associates and work community.

WEALTH

7. a) I am comfortable with my financial situation and feel self empowered.
   b) same as above

FUTURE/REPUTATION

8. a) I have clearly defined my future goals.

b) I have a good reputation in my business and am achieving my goals.

Pay particular attention to the questions that you rated from (0-3). Make a list of these areas of concern. Refer to the Pa Kua grid in chapter three. Overlay the grid on your floor plan by lining up compass direction of the Pa Kua to the compass direction of your home. The eight pie shaped sections of the Pa Kua relate to the eight life aspirations. Work only on the areas of your life that need to be fixed. For example if you rated your career as a 2 then refer to the north sector of the Pa Kua.

3. REMOVE CLUTTER, CLEAR BLOCKS AND PROPER MAINTENANCE

CLUTTER

Begin by removing the clutter from areas of concern. Clutter stagnates the flow of energy in a space. Every item, object and thought is attached to us by a tiny thread and pulls and tugs at our every thought. A good rule to remember is that if you don't need it, like it or want it, get rid of it. Look inside your closets, cupboards, under beds and behind doors, under the stairs, in the garage and in the back yard. If you are deeply attached to some of your items and have difficulty discarding them, store them in plastic, see through tubs and put them away in a storage area.

BLOCKS

Blocks are items or objects that stop the flow of energy. These items and objects are particularly inauspicious on pathways, entrances, windows, hallways and foyers. For example, if you are faced with the side view of a large wall unit upon entering a front entrance the area becomes stale and blocked creating an un welcoming feeling. When the view from a window is a brick wall or large obstruction it creates an oppressed feeling. When the block cannot be removed, create a diversion or soften the effect by using plants, screens or a window dressing treatment.

MAINTENANCE

The outside of your home or office reflects how you feel about yourself. First impressions are usually lasting impressions so keep the outside of your building well maintained. Remove weeds, dead plants and fallen branches, fill in holes, cracks, and discard or fix all damaged objects and items. Replace old roof tiles and remove peeling paint from windowsills and walls. Replace all burnt out bulbs. Be sure that the front entrance has a bright bulb. Most important of all be sure your front door opens and closes properly.

Maintaining the inside of a building is equally important as the outside. When the inside walls, windows, doors and ceilings and plumbing are cracked, rusted or falling apart it creates feelings of stagnation and staleness, resulting in a lack of energy for those living around it. Burnt out bulbs, broken furniture and appliances that aren't working create unrest and an anxious feeling making the occupant feel frustrated, tired and lifeless. Keeping the inside of your space in good repair and in working order allows the chi energy to flow freely.

4. ORIENTING THE GRID AND YOUR PERSONAL KUA

Use the Pa Kua to locate which area of your home relates to areas of your life. When possible rooms can be selected according to the grid. For example a perfect location for your office would be in the career or wealth area of your home. Be aware that all of these areas are connected to a compass direction, elements and colours. To keep balance and harmony select colours items and objects and patterns that best reflect the area of the Pa Kua. The grid can be a valuable tool in helping restore balance in your life.

Refer to the cycles of the five elements to help put balance back into a space that is out of balance. An example of this would be when a room has too much blue (water) use the reducing cycle of the elements and add wood (green) to reduce the energy of the water. If there is too much fire energy in a room use earth (brown) to reduce its affect or you can use the domination cycle and bring in the element of water (blue or black) to overpower the fire energy. The cycle of creation is used to keep things in balance. If you want to add colours and design a space use the creative cycle of the elements to keep things in harmony. If you would like to decorate a room in earth tones use fire and metal to complement the tones. Fire creates earth and earth creates metal. All of these elements are connected and work well together.

Use the Kua charts in this book to identify your own personal Kua number and find which are your personal best directions. Once you set your goals position yourself in your best directions and avoid sitting or sleeping in your inauspicious directions. Use

the guidelines and tips in this book to avoid positioning yourself in line with negative energies such as poison arrows or under beams or directly lined up with
the door.

Once you know your Kua number you can
determine if you are in harmony with your front door,
refer to chart # on the appendix.

5. POSITIONING OF FURNITURE, OBJECTS AND SELF

Furniture should be positioned in a manner
that allows the chi to flow freely around all sides. If
you have too much furniture, relocate what you don't
use, like or need.

Make sure that the furniture is not pushed up
against the wall or arranged too closely together.
Whenever possible sofas and chairs should be positioned backing on to a wall, not with the back to an
entrance or window. Cover up any poison arrows or
sharp edges, protruding corners by covering them up
or softening them with plants. (see cures section)

Check the colours, pattern and shape of the
furniture and balance the elements to create harmony in the room. For example, if the sofa were low
square, brown and heavy it would be an earth element. Earth is very yin energy and makes you feel
grounded. If this were not your goal for the room then

you would need to balance and uplift the energy of the room by adding fire shapes and colours.

Position objects pictures and other items according to their significance. For example certificates are best in the career or future locations and if you want to attract a love interest put things in pairs and in your relationship area.

Position yourself in the power area of a room when self empowerment is needed. The power area is the farthest corner away from the door. By positioning yourself in this area you have the most advantage over the room. In the case where there are two doors consider the one that is most used and keep the other door closed or blocked.

6. APPLYING CURES AND ACTIVATING SECTORS

Once all of the clutter and blocks have been removed from an area it is time to apply remedies and cures and activate. Cure problematic areas by using suggestions outlined in the cure section of the book. Then begin to activate areas of concern by adding special objects, or items that have meaning and bring energy to the space in question.

To cure and activate a missing area of a room or space use the following method. If the area is missing from a room and has a protruding wall that faces into the space, remedy it by putting a plant or softening the affect of the edge. In the case where the missing area rests in the back or front yard use lights, shrubs, plants or decorative stones to finish or square off the area. Be sure the area is free of clutter and well maintained. If the missing area is one of the areas that you rated low be sure to activate it by adding some bright lights, water or something to add life to it such as a bird bath or bird feeder.

Refer to the cure chapter and the appendix section as guides to help select cures. Time should be taken to carefully select the cures and remedies that you feel comfortable with.

Develop your own personal insights by reading and using the I Ching Divination section in this book. Use your intuition to guide you and if something does not feel right then don't do it.

Always try to use all the senses to activate cures in a space. Use smell, colour, sound and even taste to add positive energy to a space. Use the charts in the back of this book for a quick reference to colour and scents.

7. GOING WITH THE FLOW

The final step in Feng Shui is the simplest of all. Your attitude and intention can make the difference between failure and success. If you think it won't work then you are probably right. If your intentions are to hurt someone else to benefil yourself, you will surely fail. Positive attitude and pure intention will bring you favourable results.

While going through all of the steps think of how balance and harmony can enhance your life and the life of others. Feng Shui is not a magic genie that can be summoned every time you need help. Rather, it is a way of living life in harmony simply by using the energies of nature.

Finally, apply the Taoist theory of Wu Wei, the law of "non doing". Make all of the necessary changes then let go. Things will happen naturally and in their own time. If you are too anxious and try to force things to happen you will be going against the grain. Simply sit back, relax and go with the flow.

APPENDIX

APPENDIX 1
THE FIVE ELEMENTS AND THEIR CHARACTERISTICS

ELEMENT	DIRECTION	COLOUR	SHAPE	EXPRESSES	OBJECTS
WOOD	East	Green	Rectangle	Growth, Nourishment, Creativity	Plants, Flowers, Trees
FIRE	South	Red	Triangle	Action, Energy, Danger, Power	Stove, Furnace,
EARTH	SW/NE Centre	Brown, Beige	Square	Stability, Reliability, Safety	Earth, Stones, Bricks, Clay Pots
METAL	West	White, Grey Reflective	Round	Reflection, Restraint, Precision	Coins, Sword, Mirrors
WATER	North	Blue, Black	Curved Undulating	Relaxation Communication	Fountains, Ponds

APPENDIX 2
THE PA KUA

SECTION	COLOUR	SHAPES	OBJECTS	DIRECTION
KNOWLEDGE Wisdom	Blue, Green, Earthtones	Curved, Rectangle	Books, Magazines, Pictures of Mountains	Northeast
CAREER Self	Blue, Green, White	Curved	Office Equipment Charts, Aquarium	North
MENTORS Helpful People	Blue, White, Violet	Curved, Round	Pictures or Statues of Angels, Saints, teachers or Guides	Northwest
CHILDREN Creativity	White, Blue Earthtones	Round	Pictures of children, Crafts & Artwork, Piano, Windchimes	West
RELATIONSHIP Marriage	Red, Earthtones	Traingle, Square	Paired objects, candles, Plants & flowers	Southwest
FUTURE Fame	Red, Green, Earthtones	Triangle	Trophies, certificates, Crystal, Lights, Plants	South
WEALTH Power	Green, Red	Rectangle	Crystal, Flowers, fountains, fish bowl, Items of value	Southeast
FAMILY Community	Green, Blue, Red	Rectangle	Family & Ancestor group pictures, plants, fountain	East

APPENDIX 3
PERSONAL KUA NUMBER

BIRTH YEAR	MALE	FEMALE	BIRTH YEAR	MALE	FEMALE
1920	8	7	1966	7	8
1921	7	8	1967	6	9
1922	6	9	1968	2	1
1923	2	1	1969	4	2
1924	4	2	1970	3	3
1925	3	3	1971	2	4
1926	2	4	1972	1	8
1927	1	8	1973	9	6
1928	9	6	1974	8	7
1929	8	7	1975	7	8
1930	7	8	1976	6	9
1931	6	9	1977	2	1
1932	2	1	1978	4	2
1933	4	2	1979	3	3
1934	3	3	1980	2	4
1935	2	4	1981	1	8
1936	1	8	1982	9	6
1937	9	6	1983	8	7
1938	8	7	1984	7	8
1939	7	8	1985	6	9
1940	6	9	1986	2	1
1941	2	1	1987	4	2
1942	4	2	1988	3	3
1943	3	3	1989	2	4
1944	2	4	1990	1	8
1945	1	8	1991	9	6
1946	9	6	1992	8	7
1947	8	7	1993	7	8
1948	7	8	1994	6	9
1949	6	9	1995	2	1
1950	2	1	1996	4	2
1951	4	2	1997	3	3
1952	3	3	1998	2	4
1953	2	4	1999	1	8
1954	1	8	2000	9	6
1955	9	6	2001	8	7
1956	8	7	2002	7	8
1957	7	8	2003	6	9
1958	6	9	2004	2	1
1959	2	1	2005	4	2
1960	4	2	2006	3	3
1961	3	3	2007	2	4
1962	2	4	2008	1	8
1963	1	8	2009	9	6
1964	9	6	2010	8	7
1965	8	7			

APPENDIX 4
KUA NUMBER DOOR DIRECTION

DIRECTION OF FRONT DOOR	KUA NUM	HARMONY (H) CONFLICT (C)	TO REMEDY ADD COLOUR
NORTH	1	H	-
	2	C	WHITE
	3	H	-
	4	H	-
	5	C	WHITE
	6	H	-
	7	H	-
	8	C	WHITE
	9	C	BLUE, GREEN
SOUTH	1	C	GREEN, BLUE
	2	H	-
	3	H	-
	4	H	-
	5	H	-
	6	C	EARTHTONES
	7	C	EARTHTONES
	8	H	-
	9	H	-
EAST	1	H	-
	2	C	RED
	3	H	-
	4	H	-
	5	C	RED
	6	C	BLUE, BLACK
	7	C	BLUE, BLACK
	8	C	RED
	9	H	-
WEST	1	H	-
	2	H	-
	3	C	BLUE, BLACK
	4	C	BLUE, BLACK
	5	H	-
	6	H	-
	7	H	-
	8	H	-
	9	H	-

APPENDIX 4 - page 2
KUA NUMBER DOOR DIRECTION

DIRECTION OF DOOR	KUA NUM	HARMONY (H) CONFLICT (C)	TO REMEDY ADD COLOUR	FRONT
NORTHEAST	1	C	WHITE	
	2	H	-	
	3	C	RED	
	4	C	RED	
	5	H	-	
	6	H	-	
	7	H	-	
	8	H	-	
	9	H	-	
NORTHWEST	1	H	-	
	2	H	-	
	3	C	BLUE, BLACK	
	4	C	BLUE, BLACK	
	5	H	-	
	6	H	-	
	7	H	-	
	8	H	-	
	9	C	BROWN	
SOUTHEAST	1	H	-	
	2	C	RED	
	3	H	-	
	4	H	-	
	5	C	RED	
	6	C	BLUE, BLACK	
	7	C	BLUE, BLACK	
	8	C	RED	
	9	H	-	
SOUTHWEST	1	C	WHITE	
	2	H	-	
	3	C	RED	
	4	C	RED	
	5	H	-	
	6	H	-	
	7	H	-	
	8	H	-	
	9	H	-	

APPENDIX 5
COLOUR

Red Happiness, prosperity, inspirational, exciting, powerful and energetic.

Yellow Positive, optimism, cheerful, elevating, stimulating and brighting

Green Peace, tranquility, harmony, soothing, restful, relaxing, growth, immaturity, nurturing and reju venating.

Blue Optimism, security, thoughtfulness, constancy, true, calming, introspective, responsible, tran quil, spirituality,intuition, isolation, adventure, independent, investigative, mysterious and uniqueness.

Violet Spirituality, high ideals, wonder, restful, creativity, idealism, mysticism and inspirational.

Gold Dignity, money, honour, fame, positive, optimistic, dignified, good luck and wealth.

White Purity, brightness, innocence, untainted, godli ness,cleanliness and freshness.

Black Intensity, formality, sophistication, gloomy, dynamic, money, mystery, independence, intrigue, strength and solidarity.

APPENDIX 6
SCENT

Lavender Relaxation, calm, serene, peaceful, tranquility, comfort, soothing, restful, protection and healing.

Jasmine Sensual, harmony, exotic, optimism, well-being, soothing, balancing, euphoric, comforting, inspirational, confidence, good luck in love wealth, aphrodisiac,alleviates depression and tension and raises self esteem.

Chamomile Soothing, sedative, relaxing, balancing, diss olves negativity, calming and stress-relieving.

Eucalyptus Stimulating, clearing, refreshing, cooling, purify, disinfecting, energizing and uplifting.

Lemon Cleanliness, freshness, stimulating, purifying, refreshing, energetic, motivating, positive, uplifting and clearing.

Orange Warming, uplifting, refreshing, energizing, cleansing, rejuvenating, joyful, purification, healing, abundance and happiness.

Patchouli Aphrodisiac, relaxing, balancing, uplifting, stim ulating, purifies and prosperity.

Peppermint Cooling, refreshing, stimulating, purifies, attracts positive energies, revitalizes and rejuvenates.

Rosemary Refreshing, stimulating, alleviates mental and physical fatigue, clearing, peaceful, contentment, attracts love, healing and rejuvenates.

Ylang Ylang Aphrodisiac, calming, peaceful and relaxing

APPENDIX 7
NUMBERS

1. honour and luck

2. double luck, double happiness, good number

3. unbalanced, unstable, can mean growth

4. death, change, should be combined with a lucky number

5. denotes balance, transformation and fullness

6. denotes the six emotions, sexual union, spiritual dimensions

7. seven planets, seven days of the week, seven ages, lucky number

8. luck, power, wealth and great wisdom

9. strength, long life and perception

10. fullness, completeness, longevity

GLOSSARY

Chi
Vital life force or energy that exists in everything in the cosmos. That which propels all in motion.

Compass School
The Feng Shui school that uses compass to determine the flow of chi at any given time in any given location.

Confucius
The name of a Chinese philosopher who studied the I Ching his entire life.

Elements
The Elements Wood, Fire, Earth, Metal and Water, according to the Chinese provide valuable information for the practice of Feng Shui.

Feng
Chinese character that means wind.

Shui
Chinese character that means water.

Feng Shui
Translated it means Wind Water. The Chinese Art of Placement. Harnessing the earth's natural energy and rhythms to achieve balance and harmony in a living space.

Form School
The Feng Shui school that analyzes location and land formations to determine the flow of chi.

Geomancy
Measuring the energies of the earth.

I Ching
An ancient Chinese Text referred to as "The Book of Changes".

Kua
A number that refers to one of the eight sides of the Pa Kua. A person's Kua number can determine their best compass direction and is calculated based on their year of birth.

Lo Shu
A magic square containing 9 numbers that adds up to 15 in any direction. When placed over the Pa Kua its numbers refer to various directions and aspirations.

Luo Pan
A Chinese Feng Shui compass used to determine good chi directions and times.

Pa Kua
Also referred to as Ba Gua is an eight-sided trigram used to identify the implied meaning of space within an environment.

Poison Arrow
Also referred to as "secret arrow, sha chi" and "shars". A sharp edge or obstruction with sharp chi is directed towards a home or its occupant. The inauspicious fast moving chi creates negative energy.

Sha
Stagnant chi.

Tao
"The Way" or way of living life based on Taoist philosophy.

Taoism
The philosophical system based on an ancient text.

Trigram
Three lines that are either broken or solid. When grouped in threes symbolize the combining of heaven, earth and man.

Yang
Active energy, one of two complimentary opposites and is the opposite of yin.

Yin
Passive energy, one of two complimentary opposites and is the opposite of yang.

BIBLIOGRAPHY

Collins Gem, Chinese Astrology, HARPER GEMS PUB. LON-
DON, 1996   ISBN 0-00-472296-5

Gallagher, Winifred, The Power of Place-How Our
Surroundings Shape Our Thoughts, Emotions, and Actions,
FIRST HARPER PERENNIAL, NEW YORK, 1994.
ISBN 0-06-097602-0

Linn, Denise, Sacred Space, BALLANTINE BOOKS, NEW
YORK, 1995.   ISBN 0-345-39769-X

Page, Michael, The Power of Chi, EQUARIAN PRESS, SAN
FRAN.1988   ISBN 1-85538-363-2

Pearson, David, The New Natural House Book - FIRESIDE,
NY., 1998.   ISBN 0-684-84733-7

Rossbach, Sarah and Yun, Lin, Living Color - Master Lin
Yun's Guide to Feng Shui and the Art of Color, KODANSHA
AMERICA, NEW YORK, 1994.   ISBN 1-56836-014-2

Simons, T. Raphael, Feng Shui Step by Step,   CROWN
PUB., NY. 1996   ISBN 0-517-88794-0

Too, Lillian, The Complete Illustrated Guide To Feng Shui,
ELEMENT BOOKS, SHAFTSBURY, 1996.
ISBN 1-85230-902-4

Moran, Elizabeth, Biktashev, Val, TCIG on Feng Shui, ALPHA
BOOKS, MCMILLAN PUBLISHING, NEW YORK 1999
ISBN 0-02-863106-6

Visconti, Lina, Seven Step Feng Shui, TM PUBLICATIONS,
RICHMOND HILL, 1998.
ISBN 0-9684391-0-1

Wong, Eva, Feng-Shui- The Ancient Wisdom of
Harmonious Living for Modern Times, SHAMBALA, BOSTON,
1996.   ISBN 1-57062-100-4

6

RESOURCES

BOOKS

Gallagher, Winifred, The Power of Place-How Our
Surroundings Shape Our Thoughts, Emotions, and Actions,
FIRST HARPER PERENNIAL, NEW YORK, 1994.
ISBN 0-06-097602-0

Page, Michael, The Power of Chi, EQUARIAN PRESS, SAN
FRANCISCO 1988 ISBN 1-85538-363-2

Visconti, Feng Shui, Going With The Flow
TM PUBLICATIONS, RICHMOND HILL, 1998.
ISBN 9684392-1-X

Wong, Eva, Feng-Shui- The Ancient Wisdom of
Harmonious Living for Modern Times, SHAMBALA, BOSTON,
1996. ISBN 1-57062-100-4

VIDEO

Simply Feng Shui, the art of placement
ISBN 0-9684391-2-8

MAGAZINES

Feng Shui for Modern Living
STEPHEN SKINNER, LONDON, ENGLAND

WEBSITES

www.fengshuicdn.com

www.qi-whiz.com

www.shambhallafenngshui.com

www.168fengshui.com

INSTRUCTION

*Professional Training Programs

*Online Courses contact

Website: www.fengshuicdn.com

Feng Shui Institute of Canada

9251-8 Yonge Street, Unit 121 Richmond Hill,

(Greater Toronto Area)

Ontario, Canada L4C 9T3

Tel: 416-878-5617 Email: enerchi@yesic.com

ORDER FORM

To order product please fill in form below and submit to

TM Publications, 9251-8 Yonge Street, Unit 121,

Richmond Hill, Ontario Canada L4C 9T3

BOOKS

****Seven Step Feng Shui* by Lina Visconti revised edition

ISBN #ISBN 0-9684391-3-6 $19.50 plus taxes/shipping and handling

****Feng Shui, Going With The Flow* by Lina Visconti

ISBN 0-9684391-1-X $18.50 plus taxes/shipping and handling

VIDEO

****Simply Feng Shui, the art of Placement*

ISBN 09685391-2-8 $29.00 plus taxes/shipping and handling

Check off number of copies you would like to order

☐ Seven Step Feng Shui, revised edition 19.50 each plus taxes=

☐ Feng Shui, Going With The Flow 19.50 each plus taxes =

☐ Simply Feng Shui, the art of placement (Video) 29.00 plus taxes =

Add $7.50 shipping fee in Canada, $8.50 in the USA, $10. Overseas

Name: _____ Tel:_____

Email _____ Fax_____

Address _____

City _____Country_____

Postal/Zip Code _____